CELTIC

CELTIC

Ian Archer

HAMLYN

Above *Jock Stein in an informal moment at a
training session in the early 1970s.*

Endpapers *A wide-angle view of Celtic Park.*

Title page *Frank McAvennie (by left-hand post)
scores the winner in the 1988 Scottish Cup final
against Dundee United.*

Pages 10/11 *Centre forward Steve Chalmers eludes
Rangers' skipper John Greig and shoots in the 1969
Scottish Cup final.*

Contents

Early Years 12

The Jock Stein Era 28

McNeill the Manager 48

Parkhead Heroes 58

Great Matches 92

The Record 121

Index 124

Published in 1988 by
The Hamlyn Publishing Group Limited,
a division of The Octopus Publishing Group,
Michelin House, 81 Fulham Road, London SW3 6RB,
and distributed for them by
Octopus Distribution Services Limited,
Rushden, Northamptonshire NN10 9RZ

ISBN 0 600 558 851

Printed in Spain

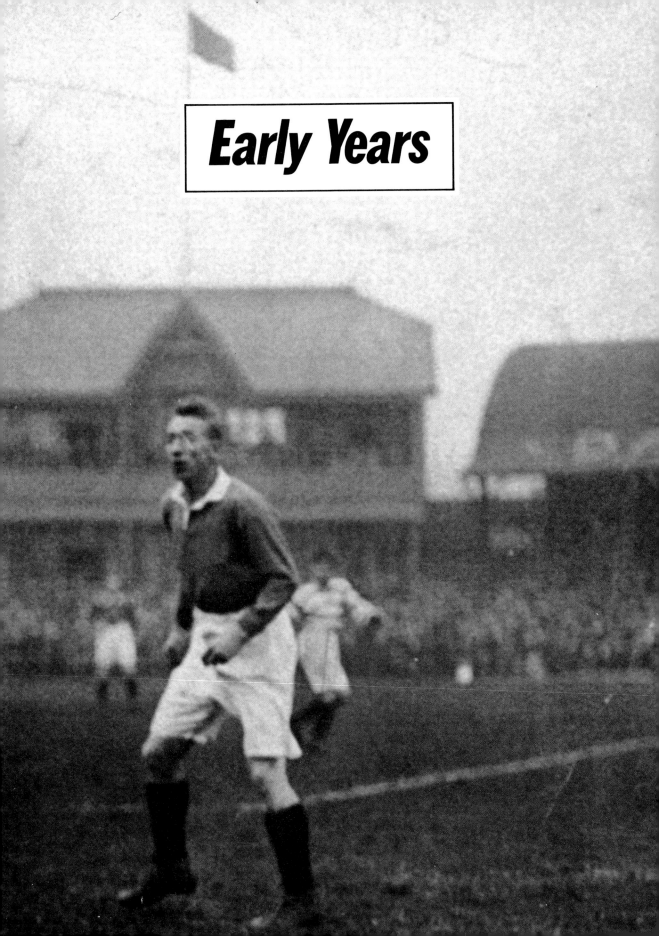

Early Years

Above *James Kelly, Celtic's first great star, signed in 1885.*

Preceding pages *Jimmy McStay, Celtic captain in the late Twenties and early Thirties, clears the ball with an overhead kick out of defence.*

If faith and hope have sustained Celtic for one hundred years, it was charity which was the reason for the club's start. Packed into Glasgow's East End at the height of the industrial revolution were thousands of Irish Catholics, many of whom had emigrated to flee the great potato famine. Funds were always needed to help the poor of the parish. A football club could raise money – so a football club had to be formed. A circular letter was sent out, under the heading 'Celtic Football Club':

'The above club was formed in November 1887 by a number of Catholics in the East End of the city. The main object of the club is to supply the East End conferences of the St Vincent de Paul Society with the funds for the maintenance of the Dinner Tables for our needy children in the missions of St Mary's, St Michael's and Sacred Heart. Many cases of sheer poverty are left unaided through lack of means. It is therefore with this principal object that we have set afloat the "Celtic" and we invite you as one of our ever-ready friends to assist us in putting our new park in proper working order for the coming football season.'

The guiding light of this enterprise was a man called Andrew Kerins, from Ballymote in County Sligo, who was better known as Brother Wilfred of the Marists and Headmaster of the Sacred Heart School. He was full of enthusiasm for football. His school children played the game and he had organised matches in aid of charity. The country's first Catholic-based club, Edinburgh Hibernian, had been formed in the capital in 1875 and had attracted support in the West of Scotland. It was thought that Glasgow should have a Catholic club of its own.

In 1887, Hibs had knocked Dumbarton out of the Scottish Cup and on their way home had been waylaid in Glasgow. Their secretary John McFadden suggested that a club similar to his own should be formed in the East End. Hibs had already played there in front of a 12,000 crowd in a charity match.

Under the guidance of Brother Wilfred, Celtic began to get themselves organised. A week after a first meeting, a ground was leased for an annual rent of £50 a year. 'Ground' is probably the wrong word: the piece of derelict land on the Gallowgate had to be transformed and every night in the winter of 1887 hundreds of volunteers cleared away the stones, so that by May of 1888, the first match was able to be played on it.

Edinburgh Hibs and Cowlairs played a goal-less friendly, and a 5,000 crowd was able to see the little stadium that had been created. There was a small stand with the dressing rooms underneath it. There were nine separate gates but children could watch for free from the wall of the adjacent cemetery. Entrance was sixpence, ladies free. Within six months of formation, Celtic were ready to play football.

To do so, they needed a team. And of all the masterstrokes in the transfer market that Jock Stein was to pull almost a century later, none could have matched for impudence or audacity the very first signing that the club made: they went out and acquired Scotland's best player!

James Kelly was the centre half of Renton, a club which had already pronounced themselves to be 'Champions of the World' after defeating West Bromwich Albion in the earlier part of 1888. This was not hyperbole. The teams had won their respective Cups and, after all, only England and Scotland were playing the game at this time.

As an amateur Kelly could play for anyone. He turned out for Edinburgh Hibs before arriving at Celtic Park. His signature was crucial because the new club had gained official recognition. And within months six other players arrived from the same club, and Celtic were never to look back.

Celtic played their first match – against Rangers – on 28 May 1888. No-one

could possible have realized that their intial match inaugurated what would become one of the biggest rivalries in world sport. Celtic were just starting, Rangers, despite being in existence since 1873, had not yet challenged the big clubs. It was billed as a friendly and that was exactly what it was.

Rangers, in fact, fielded mostly a reserve side, but Celtic showed no mercy and won 5-2, the honour of scoring the club's first-ever goal falling to Neil McCallum. Afterwards the teams repaired to the nearby St Mary's Hall, where they had supper, were entertained by a concert and participated 'in several toasts.' In other words, they had a party! A local sporting paper commented: 'Financially, Dumbarton or Queen's Park might have pleased treasurer Maley better, but for a genuine good match, the Light Blues (Rangers) are favourites with the Parkhead crowd'.

Some 2,000 had watched the first game. Two weeks later there were three times that number for the match against Dundee Harp. In the rest of the season Celtic played two more games, Clyde gaining the distinction of being the first club to beat them. In effect these were all training matches as the club geared up for 1888–89, their first season in competitive football.

That first season was not without controversy, or success. In fact Celtic reached the final of the Scottish Cup, beating Shettleston, Cowlairs, Albion Rovers and St Bernards in the early rounds. They then lost 0-1 to Clyde but Willie Maley, effectively the manager of the club, protested that Celtic's opponents had turned up late and that the final minutes of the game had been played in darkness. He won that appeal and the furious Clyde had to play again. They refused to change in the Celtic pavilion, turned up already kitted out and were trounced 9-2.

Celtic's 1907–8 side, which won the championship for the fourth successive year. Long-serving Willie Maley, who had effectively managed the club since 1888, is at left.

Patsy Gallacher, one of the greatest inside forwards in the history of the Scottish League, starred for Celtic in the years before and after the First World War.

Two more wins against East Stirlingshire and Dumbarton put them into the first Scottish Cup Final in their very first season where the impressive Third Lanark awaited them. Again there was a storm. The game, played in February, was always remembered as 'The Snow Final'. The referee declared Hampden Park playable, the teams objected and eventually the match was played as a friendly – although nobody bothered to tell the crowd. Third Lanark won 3-0; but it was closer when the sides played in the real final a week later, Celtic going down 2-3.

So Celtic were off and playing – they even went to Belfast for a couple of matches. They were attracting some of the biggest crowds in Scotland and they were able to hand over £421 16s 9d to charity, proving that they could live up to their reasons for being created. They were, however, not always popular. The reason was that the club had aggressively sought out a good team in an era when the sport was still supposed to be amateur, but which clearly wasn't. Although that money had been paid to charity, Celtic captain James Kelly had bought a pub for £650. A newspaper asked how he could so that on a joiner's wage. It hardly needed to supply an answer.

Professionalism

In fact, everyone apart from Queen's Park was paying players one way or another. Indeed in 1891, when Celtic acquired Dan Doyle from Everton, the other players threatened to go on strike unless their wages were increased. Yet under the archaic Scottish Football Association rules, they were still supposed to be playing for nothing.

To aggravate the problem, English football already allowed professionals. Yet Celtic were able to attract Scots back over the border. Their success was just one of the catalysts for the rules being changed in 1893 and that move, combined with the creation of the Scottish League, swept football into the pattern which we know today. But in those early years, under-the-counter payments, frequent bans and the expulsion of clubs whose books did not add up were the stock-in-trade of sporting news.

It was Celtic's John McLaughlin, their SFA representative, who was the biggest advocate for change : 'You might as well attempt to stop the flow of Niagara with a kitchen chair as to endeavour to stem the tide of professionalism,' he said.'With veiled professionalism, players are masters of the clubs and can go and debauch themselves without being called into account. Under the new system, the clubs will be masters of the players and the standard of play will rise.'

That was all to happen and Celtic would be at the forefront of Scottish football for the next century. But in the meantime they were not prepared to be patient. By 1891–2, they were ready to grasp the Scottish Cup for the first time. Not content with that they also won the Glasgow Cup and the Charity Cup and so did the treble.

In the Scottish Cup Final, Celtic played Queen's Park, a clash between the two philosophies in the game. The newer club had brought thousands to football who had previously never been interested in the game. But the authorities underestimated the demand and were not ready to cope with the massive 40,000 crowd which assembled at Ibrox Park.

Despite the presence of 150 policemen, including four on horseback, the crowd kept on spilling over on to the pitch. The game was held up on several occasions and during the first half the club officials met and decided the game should be reduced to the status of a friendly. That meant that Campbell's goal for Celtic, the only one of the match after 60 minutes, did not count.

The Final was put back for a week to allow Rangers to construct extra terraces but an SFA decision to double the admission prices cut the next crowd to 22,000. The outcome of the match was crucial to the history of the Scottish game because Celtic, who had been playing League football, routed Queen's Park 5-1. The amateurs could never hope to compete with the 'professionals.'

Campbell scored twice, as did McMahon, Celtic's other score coming from an own goal. It released a spontaneous show of affection among the slums of Glasgow's East End. The bands turned out and the people took to the streets as the Celtic team returned from Ibrox on the other side of the city.

By the turn of the century, Celtic had won the Scottish Cup three times, the Championship on four occasions, the Glasgow Cup four times and the Charity Cup six times. In 1895, they had set a League record when they beat Dundee 11-0 at Parkhead.

They were responsible for innovations. They had forced the SFA to introduce goal nets, at least for the semi-finals and finals of the Cup, after an incident in the 1893 final when Queen's Park won with a goal which Celtic claimed had never crossed the line. In the same year they pioneered floodlights. They strung gas lights on a dozen wooden posts 50 feet high; the trouble was, the system sagged and stopped the flight of the ball. They covered their pitch with straw and tarpaulins in the worst of the winter. Their first decade brought them instant success, although there were mutterings that the original charitable aims had begun to take second place as the club went all out for success on the field.

They had improved their Parkhead ground immensely. In 1898, they were hosts for the World Cycling Championships, having built a special cement track for the occasion. Celtic Park was recognised as a stadium suitable for Scotland's international matches, the most famous being the Rosebery International of 1900, named after the Earl who attended that day. Scotland played not in their traditional shirts but in his Lordship's racing colours. By then the ground could hold 70,000, was the biggest in the world, and Celtic could say that, after only 12 years of existence, they had truly arrived.

The Edwardian Age

All of today's Celtic supporters would say that the club's most successful period came under Jock Stein, when they captured not only the European Cup but also won nine successive Scottish Championships. They would probably be right. But there was another Golden Age which coincided, aptly, with those last peaceful years before the First World War changed everything.

Starting in 1905, Celtic won six successive championships and it was not just that record which mirrored what happened 70 years later. If there is a common thread between the two achievements, it lies in the fact that, at both times, the club had decided that they would try to rear their own players.

From the first-ever signing of James Kelly from Renton to start the new team, Celtic had plundered remorselessly, both in the days when it was, strictly speaking, illegal to do so and also in the times when professionalism permitted it. As probably the wealthiest club in Scotland, if not in Great Britain, it made sense to do so, especially after Celtic had been formed into a limited liability company in 1897.

But Willie Maley, now the undisputed manager at Celtic Park and in control of all team matters, had not been alone in wondering if the star players had always given good value. One of the best of them in the 1890s was Dan Doyle, who was persuaded to come north from Everton. He was a likeable mercenary who in fact had played for nine different clubs before he came to Glasgow. He was not the easiest of men to discipline and had once failed to show up for a cup-tie which was lost at non-League Arthurlie, still one of the biggest upsets in the history of that competition. He was fined £5. Round about that time, it was decided to have some kind of youth policy.

Gradually Maley collected around him some of the finest young talent the club were ever to have. Jimmy Quinn came from Smithson Albion in 1901. Jimmy McMenemy came from Rutherglen Glencairn, joined a few months later by a team-mate, centre forward Alec Bennett. Other youngsters included goalkeeper Davy Adams, Jim Young and Alex McNair, from Stenhousemuir.

The Scottish Referee, the most influential of the sporting papers, noted: 'In previous years we have become accustomed to announce important captures from some English club or other but this season there are none; and here we think the directors have given further proof of their wisdom. It is to Junior Talent that they now direct their attention . . .'.

But transforming youthful promise into professional ability is never an easy or a quick process. Maley was forced to admit that 1902–3 was 'the

Celtic's 1913–14 team, with manager Maley in boater. This side won the first of four consecutive championships.

most disheartening season in the club's history and the worst in terms of results.' But he did not have to wait long until it came right. Celtic won the 1904 Cup final against Rangers in front of a 65,000 crowd at Hampden Park. It was an astonishing match in which Rangers were two goals up and were then beaten by a Quinn hat-trick. Celtic were on the verge of their six winning seasons and Maley was proud to reveal that his team had cost less than £200 to acquire, most of it spent in signing-on fees for the young players.

As with all great teams, few changes were made on a week-to-week basis. Injuries would occasionally force a switch, but the side could easily slip off the supporters' lips: Adams; Watson, Orr; McNair, Loney, Hay; Bennett, McMenemy, Quinn, Somers, Hamilton. Its basis, as with any other winning side, was a sound defence.

Goalkeeper Adams was thought to have the best concentration of anyone in the game, quite an asset when for long periods in a lot of matches he had little to do. The full-backs were hard tacklers and McNair a compelling wing half, a better player when he dropped a little deeper than the inside forward role where he had started his career.

But, as always with Celtic, it was the forward line that mattered and the few surviving fans who remember the Edwardian team still consider it to be the finest the club have ever produced. On the right wing Bennett was a fast runner and the scorer of a surprising number of goals. Inside him McMenemy was the personification of a Scottish inside forward, settling on the ball, constantly changing the direction and the tempo of the game. He, too, could score goals. Quinn was a fearless centre forward, good in the air and on the ground. On the left Somers would fetch and carry, while

Hamilton was a good crosser of the ball. It was certainly the finest forward line in Scottish football up to that time.

The triumphant surge to those six titles started in the 1904–5 season. Ironically, under todays's rules, that Championship would have been won by Rangers. They finished level on points after the scheduled 26 games and had by far the better scoring record, 83-28 as opposed to Celtic's 68-31. There was a play-off at Hampden Park which Celtic won narrowly 2-1 to clinch their first title since 1898.

There was another similarity between Celtic's pre-war successes and the nine-in-a-row which came over half a century later. At both times Rangers were in a state of comparative decline. In the next three seasons, Celtic won by six points over Hearts, seven over Dundee and four over Falkirk. By then, there were 34 matches in a League campaign.

In 1906–7, Celtic won the Cup and League double, the first time that feat had been accomplished in Scottish football. One strange story illustrates that the game was different in those days. Celtic did not field a reserve side and when goalkeeper Adams cut his hand in a benefit game at Ibrox, Rangers promptly lent their rivals their own keeper. Tom Sinclair played 10 games for Celtic and had shut-outs in nine of them. He won a Glasgow Cup final medal with the Parkhead club, then returned to Rangers, where he won a Second Eleven Cup medal. And before the end of the season he was transferred to Newcastle United, where he won an English Championship medal. It could hardly happen today.

In the Cup Final against Hearts, an Orr penalty after 55 minutes, followed by two Somers goals, gave Celtic an easy win. A year later, the club added a second double in successive years when, after clinching the Championship, they beat St Mirren 5-1 in the Final. This was to be Bennett's last game. He went to Rangers, with his place being taken by Willie Kivlichan, who had been at Ibrox several years before. With the club also winning the Glasgow Cup and the Charity Cup, they took a clean sweep of all the honours.

The 1908–9 season turned out to be one of the most traumatic in the short history of Scottish football. It was the Cup final which caused all the problems. Celtic met Rangers in front of 70,000 at Hampden Park and they enjoyed a thrilling, if controversial match. A Quinn header gave Celtic an early lead, but Gilchrist equalized and Bennett, with his new club, put Rangers ahead with only 15 minutes left. Celtic stormed forward and gained a 2-2 draw with an odd goal. Their new right winger Munro tried a cross-shot which goalkeeper Rennie gathered cleanly. But as he tried to avoid Quinn, who was rushing in, the referee decided that he had carried the ball over the line.

There were no crowd troubles – but the replay was different and it was all down to a misunderstanding. The SFA rules said that in the event of a draw there would be no extra time and a third game would be played. Celtic, through Willie Maley, thought the spectators deserved a result, contacted Rangers and viewed the matter publicly. The outcome was that many in the crowd expected another 30 minutes when the game ended in a 1-1 draw, Quinn scoring again for Celtic.

Several players, mostly Celts, stayed on the field, clearly expecting extra time, but nothing happened. The crowd encroached on the field and the violence rapidly escalated. As the police sent for reinforcements, fans set a bonfire alight with whisky, burnt down the turnstiles, attacked the fire brigade and cut their hoses. The riot continued for several hours in the worst outbreak of violence so far in Scottish football.

Celtic and Rangers met to discuss the situation. They agreed a joint statement: 'Although it was mooted during the week that extra time might

The incident that led to John Thomson's death in September 1931. The keeper dived at the feet of Rangers' centre-forward Sam English and fractured his skull on English's left knee.

be played in the event of a draw, it was found that the Cup competition rules prevented this. On the account of the regrettable occurrences on Saturday, both clubs agree to petition the Association that the final tie be abandoned.' They added that, if asked to play a third game, one of them would scratch.

In the event, the SFA, by a margin of only 15-11, decided to abandon the Cup and withold the medals, the only time that has happened. They contributed £500 to Queen's Park, the owners of Hampden Park, and instructed Rangers and Celtic to pay another £150 each.

It was the biggest football scandal of the century. One of the solutions offered was that entrance money should be doubled and the game moved upmarket because 'this would exclude some thousands of hooligans who would then have sixpence to spend on buying soap to wash their faces and get their chins scraped. To clean their mouths of filthy speech would require a miracle but their exclusion would prevent the pollution of the atmosphere and ears of the ordinary man in the street'.

Celtic pulled themselves together remarkably well. After the ill-fated replay they had to play their remaining eight League games in the next 12 days and they needed 12 points to retain the title. They did so at Hamilton to make it five in a row.

Although the club added a sixth successive championship in the following season, and Alex McNair started his long run at full-back, the

cracks were beginning to show and that was the end of an era for Celtic. This is their record over that period.

It was largely achieved by the same men: McNair went on to play in 583 League games, McMenemy appeared in 453 and Quinn some 271. During the six seasons, Celtic played in 192 League games, lost only 23 and gained 305 points out of a possible 384. It was too much to hope that it would continue, but the club's decline was gradual and they even managed more, if sporadic, success before the outbreak of war.

Patsy Gallacher, still sometimes referred to 'as the greatest Celt of all', arrived in 1911 but was not in the Cup final side held to a surprising draw in front of 45,000 at Ibrox by Hamilton Accies, who had finished 16th in the League. Goals from Quinn and McAteer in the second half of the replay gave the club its seventh Cup triumph.

Twelve months later, again at Ibrox, Celtic met their neighbours Clyde in the Scottish Cup final. McMenemy scored the first goal and Gallacher, in his final debut, the second, so Willie Maley enjoyed a victory over his brother Alex, who managed Clyde. The Championship was lost to Rangers amid accusations that the fixture list was compiled to suit the Ibrox club. War was to break out – but on a football level, Celtic were ready again to dominate the Scottish game.

The First World War was a curious time for football. Newspapers campaigned for the game to be halted and that the players should all join up as a boost to national morale. In fact in the first year of war, international matches between the four home countries were stopped, as was the Scottish Cup. But the club game continued and it was a spell of domination for Celtic.

The rules were that no-one should be paid more than £2 a week for playing and that a player could not appear on a Saturday if he had not been working during the week. There were plenty of grumblings about the fact that some footballers appeared to be escaping the war effort, but they seem ill-founded. One ex-Celtic player, Willie Angus, won the VC in the trenches of France. The regular centre half Peter Johnstone was killed in action. Maley sent footballs to the front so the soldiers could have a game. Appeals to join up were made over the loudspeakers at Parkhead.

The young Patsy Gallacher was fined £3 in 1916 for bad time-keeping at his job in the shipyards and it was clearly intended to be a warning to other players. The League also suspended him for five weeks and Celtic were fined £25.

During the War, Maley rebuilt Celtic into another side which could dominate Scottish football with some ease. In the 1914–15 season, Celtic won 30 out of 38 matches, including a spell in which they dropped only one match in 19 games and did not concede a single goal.

Jimmy Quinn eventually began to drop out of the picture. His injuries had been taking longer to clear up and he had played only six times during that title conquest. Gallacher was a more than adequate replacement as a genuine star.

In 1916, Celtic rattled in a record 104 goals to win again, one curiosity being that they played twice on one Saturday, beating Raith Rovers in the morning 6-1 and then Motherwell in the afternoon 3-1. They had now been Scottish Champions 13 times in 26 seasons, a colossal achievement.

Much of the credit must go to Maley. He had been with the club over 25 years as a player, secretary and manager and was given a present of 300

Below left *Jimmy McStay with the Scottish Cup after Celtic had beaten Motherwell in the 1933 final.*

Below right *Jimmy Delaney, best-loved Celtic player of his era, joined the club as a winger in 1935. After the Second World War he moved to Manchester United, swiftly becoming an Old Trafford favourite.*

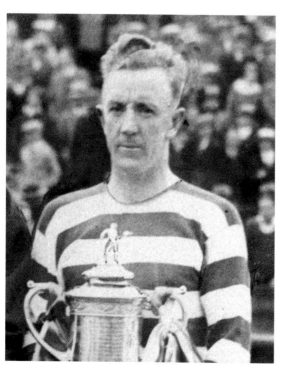

24

guineas to celebrate his silver anniversary. He had created his first young team, seen the club through a suprisingly short period of transition and then built up another side which was almost as good. There seemed nothing to stop the Celtic bandwagon from rolling on and on.

Between the Wars

Between the wars, Celtic did not have their happiest times. This, of course, is relative. Most other clubs in Scottish football would have been highly delighted to have achieved what Celtic accomplished. But standards had been set and they were not always matched during this period.

The club won the Scottish Cup in 1923, 1925, 1927, 1931, 1933 and 1937. They won the Championship in 1919, 1922, 1926 and 1936. So over the two decades they never won the double. Yet the most worrying fact was that their position as undisputed leaders in the Scottish game passed to the other side of the city – and to Rangers.

The Ibrox club had a long golden period, ironically learning a lot of their lessons from Celtic. Bill Struth became a dominating manager in the style of Maley. Unlike Celtic they ran more than one team. The failure to keep a reserve side was the root cause why Celtic lost their old consistency. Irregular disputes over bonuses hint at general disquiet at Parkhead. The fans certainly believed that the club were always reluctant to spend big money to buy success.

The thinking of Celtic during this period can be summed up by looking at the career of their greatest player of the time, centre forward Jimmy McGrory. He spanned the two decades. Between 1923 and 1937, he scored 410 League goals and 550 in all matches. It remains a Brtish goal scoring record, as does the eight he scored in one game against Dunfermline in 1928.

His most famous goals were the ones which brought Celtic the Cup in 1925 and the winner against England in 1933, the goal which established the legendary Hampden Roar.

In 1928 McGrory set off on holiday with Maley en route to Lourdes. Arsenal had already expressed an interest in the centre forward but McGrory had always been adamant that he would play out his career at Celtic. Nothing was mentioned by the manager during their break but on the way home Maley announced that Arsenal's manager, Herbert Chapman, would be coming to see him in London.

A furious McGrory allowed himself to be interviewed by Chapman, who had offered Celtic a £10,000 fee – a British record at that time. He looked for a way out and decided the only solution was to ask for so big a percentage for himself that even Arsenal would refuse. He demanded £2,000 and was turned down. He went back to Scotland with his manager, continued to score goals and said 'McGrory of Arsenal would never have sounded the same as McGrory of Celtic.' The fans wondered what sort of club would have been willing to sell their major star – and in such tawdry circumstances.

There were other fine players as well as Patsy Gallacher in the early stages: Peter Wilson, a great wing half, and the mercurial Tommy McInally, who came and went twice from Celtic Park as the club tried to control his moods – and just before the Second World War broke out, Jimmy Delaney was a constant source of delight to the Parkhead crowds.

Winning the Cup in 1923 was important to Celtic in a disappointing season because it was their tenth triumph and equalled the record of Queen's Park, a club now almost consigned to the pages of history as far as winning was concerned. In a grim defensive battle – Hibs had not conceded a goal on their way to Hampden Park – a Jimmy Cassidy header decided the outcome and gave Alex McNair, restored at the age of 39, a last honour.

Two years later, Dundee were beaten in the Final when Gallacher scored a goal by jumping across the line with the ball wedged between his feet and the young McGrory dived forward to head a second. He was up at the front of the bus with the Cup on the way home, an indication of what Maley thought of his young centre forward.

In 1927, Celtic defeated Second Division East Fife in the final, but were crushingly beaten 12 months later when Rangers ended a 25-year stretch without winning the Cup. After their side's 4-0 destruction even Celtic supporters had to admit that they were now in second place to the Ibrox club.

The death of goalkeeper John Thomson at Ibrox on 5 September 1931, when he dived at the feet of Rangers' centre forward Sam English, cast a horrible shadow over the start of the next decade. A few months before his death, Thomson had been in goal in the Cup Final when Celtic played the hugely talented Motherwell side in front of a 105,000 crowd that could hardly have believed the outcome.

Motherwell were two goals up with only eight minutes to play. Then McGrory equalised and an own goal by Motherwell centre half Alan Craig gave Celtic a second chance. They won the replay 4-2, the inevitable McGrory scoring twice.

The centre forward did the same two years later, against the same team, as another Cup victory over Motherwell gave McGrory his fourth Cup medal and Celtic's their 14th triumph in that competition. But the lean years were just around the corner. The club won the Cup again in 1937 and the League in 1936.

That 1937 game is best remembered for establishing the all-time British attendance record, some 146,433 spectators jamming into Hampden Park to watch Celtic beat Aberdeen 2-1. But in their silver jubilee season, 12 months later, they could not win an honour.

McGrory moved on to be manager of Kilmarnock and his new side came to Parkhead and promptly knocked Celtic out of the Cup in the third round before defeating Rangers in the semi-final. Alas, Kilmarnock lost in the Final to East Fife, who became the first – and last – Second Division side ever to land the trophy.

The Scottish League suspended football 'for the duration' after the declaration of war in 1939. Some divisional matches were played, players were limited to wages of £2 a week and gates were restricted for fear of bombing. For Celtic, it was the end of the Willie Maley era.

He was 71 years of age and had been at the club for 52 years. He had been given an honorarium of 2,500 guineas at the silver jubilee dinner, but became involved in a long dispute as to whether tax should be paid on it. The parting was not amicable and for 10 years he refused to return and watch a game at Celtic Park. But the news was announced on New Year's Day, 1940.

The new manager was Jimmy McStay, a former Celtic captain who had just completed a successful season with Alloa Athletic. He was never to be completely in control, as Celtic refused to take war-time football seriously. Although other clubs in Scotland fielded such guest players as Stanley Matthews and Tommy Lawton, the Celtic directors took a different view. They refused McStay permission to field Matt Busby, who had been looking for a game.

Rangers won the restricted League six times out of six during the war; but it was the falling away of Celtic which was remarkable, their own standings being 13th, 5th, 3rd, 10th, 2nd, 2nd. Although they improved in those last two years – Delaney was back – Celtic's problems in later years were put down to the way they had allowed the club to float downwards during the war.

In July 1945, McStay stepped off a tram near the ground and saw the newspaper placards announcing his dismissal. Jimmy McGrory was coming back as manager. As it happened, there was some doubt for the next 25 years as to who did actually manage the club. It was to be the era of chairman Bob (later Sir Robert) Kelly.

Sir Robert Kelly

From his appointment as chairman in 1947 until his death in 1971, Robert Kelly was 'Mr Celtic' He defended the club with pride, gloried in its successes – and brooked no interference with his will or judgment. An austere, distant man, he revelled in the club's traditions and would yield to no-one in the causes in which he believed.

Celtic was in his blood. His father was the great James Kelly, taken from Renton in the 1880s to become the man around which the new club played. In over two decades he became a stern legislator in the Scottish game but it was not until he allowed Jock Stein to take full charge of the playing side that he established himself as chairman of a Celtic club which won as many trophies as their supporters demanded.

The irony was that, in the football gates boom which followed the Second World War until the end of the Forties, Celtic attracted huge crowds but could not win either the League or the Cup. For example the Parkhead crowd for the opening match of the 1948–49 season was an immense 55,000 – against opposition which was hardly glamorous. By that Christmas, they had been watched by over a million.

That was astonishing considering that only 12 months before – and for the only time in the club's history – relegation had become more than a distinct possibility. By the start of April, they had collected only 23 points from 29 matches and in the last match of the season at Dundee they had to win to make sure that they did not go down alongside the amateurs of Queen's Park.

The Dundee directors, it is said, decided to pay their players the biggest bonus in the club's history, despite the fact that there was nothing riding on the game for them. It was a reminder that Celtic have not always had much help inside the Scottish game for all the glories they have brought to it. In the end Celtic won 3-1 with a hat-trick from Jock Weir, whom they had bought from Blackburn for £7,000 – possibly the most important signing that the club ever made. They had flirted with disaster and took immediate steps to make sure that such an embarrassment never occurred again.

In the following months, they secured two players who were to start some kind of revival at Parkhead. Bobby Collins, then an 18-year-old, was signed from Pollok Juniors after a long wrangle with the SFA and Everton, who also wanted him. They failed in a bid to bring the great English inside forward Wilf Mannion to Glasgow – but they had dug up a bit of treasure when they brought Charles Patrick Tully from Belfast Celtic for a mere £8,000.

Gradually, but it took time, Celtic were putting together a side which would see them through the Fifties. John McPhail, Willie Fernie and Bertie Peacock appeared on the scene.

Those bits of business were enough to see Celtic take the Cup in 1951, when they beat Motherwell in the Final with a single goal from McPhail in front of a 134,000 crowd. They could not add to that success in the following season, but although they did not know it at the time, a new player had arrived unheralded at the club from the Welsh outpost of Llanelli. Few remembered him playing for Albion Rovers. His name was Jock Stein.

Winger turned midfield orchestrator, Bobby Collins made his Celtic debut in 1949, played 220 games for the club and won 31 caps for Scotland. In 1958 he joined Everton and then sparked the Leeds side in the early 1960s.

The Jock Stein Era

Preceding pages *Celtic's 'double'-winning side of 1953–4. Future manager Jock Stein is second from the right in the back row.*

Opposite *Jock Stein in his playing days at Parkhead in the early Fifties.*

Jock Stein was, in all senses, a big man. For over 20 years he was the greatest figure in Scottish football and probably the best-known person in the country as well. He knew everyone and everyone thought they knew him. He was as much at home with the man on the terraces as he was at ease with the great and famous coaches and managers of Europe.

'You can't cheat them. They are the ones who understand this game,' he used to say about the fans. He worried about the quality of the entertainment they were receiving and what it cost them. Once, during a bad winter, Celtic's match at Dundee was put off at lunchtime on the Saturday. Stein sprinted to his car, drove miles and then stood shivering at the side of the motorway, flagging down the supporters' buses. He remained – despite his fame – a man of the people.

It was not hard to understand why. The three most famous managers in the history of British football – Stein, Sir Matt Busby and Bill Shankly – all came from within a 20 mile radius of each other, products of the now defunct mining villages of Lanarkshire, south of Glasgow. These were no places for airs and graces. These were small, tight, proud communities in which a man was expected to pull his weight. Stein never forgot that he came from a mining community.

Nor did he ever ignore the fact that, until he became Celtic manager, he had found football hard. As a player, he enjoyed none of the perks or the lifestyle that today's players take for granted.

Jock Stein was born on 5 October 1922, at 339 Glasgow Road, Burnbank, near Hamilton. He played football at school, his major attributes being his height and his ability to carry out instructions. After leaving at 14, he worked for a few months in a carpet factory but did not like it. Instead he went into the pits. 'I will never work with better men,' he was fond of saying a lot later.

It was inevitable that he would turn to football. His father George was on the committee of a local club, Blantyre Victoria. But Stein took a long time to fill out – 'he was a beanpole', a friend remembered – so it was a surprise when a local senior side asked him to play a trial for them at the age of 18.

Albion Rovers were then, and still are, just about the least glamorous and most unfashionable of all Scottish clubs. Their one and only moment of fame came in 1920 when they lost in the Scottish Cup final against Kilmarnock. Their tiny Cliftonhill ground, with its miniscule grandstand, was hardly the setting for the start of a great career. Even Stein knew that. He waited several days after the Rovers had approached him before signing, just in case something better turned up.

Stein now played wartime football for a maximum wage of £2 a week. He was to be part of a team which generally propped up the League and conceded 90 goals a season. It says much that the centre half did not sink without trace, but people were quietly noticing how he never gave up – and always seemed to have time to encourage those who played alongside him. He seemed to play well against the big names – men like Rangers' Jimmy Smith and St Mirren's Alex Linwood.

After the War, Rovers were in the Second Division but gained promotion in 1948 and the wages leapt to the princely sum of £5 with a £2 win bonus. They won just three games in a solitary season in the top flight. But in the souvenir brochure to commemorate the club's success, Stein was described as 'the best capture the club ever made. Strong, fearless, dependable, gives little rope to opposing centre forwards and his all-round ability and enthusiasm acts as a tonic to his mates. He acts as captain of the side - an honour richly deserved.'

The trouble was that Stein was going nowhere. Relegated, he became

*One of Celtic's most faithful
servants, skipper Billy McNeill
in the 1970s.*

disillusioned in Coatbridge. He wanted to play elsewhere. Of all places an offer arrived from Llanelli in South Wales. For a man who was to end up as manager of Celtic, it seemed a curious detour to make. Oddly, it was also the most important.

For the first time Stein was full-time professional, paid £12 a week, but he was far from happy. His wife Jean had stayed behind in Lanarkshire and twice her house had been burgled. He was on the way to tell Llanelli that he wanted to go back to Scotland when the club chairman met him in the street with the news, 'Celtic want you.'

It was the transfer that was to change his life and the course of Scottish football, but in 1951 it made little impact. He was not expected to gain a place in the first team; rather he was a useful addition to the staff in an era when it was not unusual for clubs to employ over 50 players every season. Not for the first time, though, Stein proved that, on top of all his other qualities, he was also a lucky man.

In his first week at Parkhead, the two other centre halves, Jimmy Mallan and Alec Boden, were both injured. He played against St Mirren in December, well enough to keep his place for a month. He regained the top spot in the middle of February and until he stopped playing four years later, he was never out of the side, apart from injury.

In 1953, Celtic won the Coronation Cup, beating Arsenal, Manchester United and then Hibs in a Hampden Park final watched by a 108,000 crowd. It was a watershed for the club, which won the League and Cup double the following season. At the heart of it was the unheralded figure of Stein.

In 1954, a wise decision by the Celtic chairman Robert Kelly was to further shape Stein's future. He sent the entire first team off to Switzerland to watch the final stages of the World Cup. It opened his eyes to the world game, especially the Hungarians, whom he much admired. He also had to endure sitting in the stands seeing Scotland being beaten 7-0 by Uruguay.

Never an insular person, he at once appreciated that while football in

Scotland was an enormously popular game, its standards were not necessarily very high. That search for perfection continued for the next 13 years until the day in 1967 when Celtic won the European Cup and the manager had finally found the Holy Grail.

In 1955, his career came to an end as a player. He sustained a bad ankle injury in a match against Rangers. He fought strongly for fitness but at 34 had to concede defeat. He made one appearance in 1956 in a friendly against Coleraine but he had known for some time that he was finished.

He had been far too valuable a player and, more importantly, as an influence on others, to be allowed to leave Parkhead. The club offered him the post of coaching the club's reserves. He did so happily for four years, coming into touch for the first time with youngsters who were to form the backbone of the side which swept everything before it a decade later – Billy McNeill, John Clark, Steve Chalmers and Bertie Auld. But it became clear that the fresh ideas he was bringing to the training ground were not enough to satisfy his ambitions. He needed to be a manager.

He was given a job that few others would have wanted. Dunfermline Athletic were almost terminally ill when he took over on 14 March 1960. They needed to win their last six League games to avoid relegation. Under Stein they did just that, and it is tempting to say that this might almost stand as his greatest achievement. Had they dropped into the Second Division, the manager's career might have been over before it started.

But during that spring, Stein started with a 3-2 win over Celtic, then inflicted Kilmarnock's first loss in 21 matches before winning against St Mirren, Airdrie, Clyde and Stirling Albion. It was pure Houdini stuff, the best winning streak in the club's history.

But that was only a start. It was the following season in which Stein put down his marker as a quite exceptional manager. Quite simply, Dunfermline won the Scottish Cup – and they beat Celtic in the Final.

It took two matches to do it. On the Saturday, in front of a Hampden Park crowd of 113,328, they forced a goalless draw, playing with virtually ten men for all but 12 minutes of the match. In the replay, goals by the reserve centre forward David Thomson and Charlie Dickson gave Dunfermline their first ever Cup triumph and left Celtic empty-handed for a fourth successive season. It was no wonder that Stein was invited to speak to the town from the balcony of the City Chambers when the Cup came back to Fife.

That Cup win was important because it allowed Stein to sample directly the delights – and the pitfalls – of European football for the first time. In his first season, Dunfermline beat St Patrick's Athletic and Vardar Skopje before going out of the Cup-Winners' Cup against Ujpest Dosza of Hungary. They had lost only 4-3 in Budapest but failed 0-1 at East End Park on a night when a record 24,000 turned out to watch them.

In subsequent seasons, Dunfermline were to beat Everton in the Fairs Cup and only just lose to Valencia, pulling back a four-goal deficit from the first match and taking the tie to a third game on the supposedly neutral territory of Portugal – events which caused UEFA to introduce the 'away goal' rules.

More importantly, Dunfermline had established themselves as regular First Division material. They had built a new stand, had installed improved floodlights and earned the respect of all Scottish football. It was an exercise in resurrecting a defunct club which Stein never needed to repeat, but to this day you will find people who consider his triumphs at East End Park comparable to anything he achieved with Celtic.

But after four years, it was time to move on. In April 1964, he went to Hibernian, who had been chasing him unsuccessfuly through his time in Fife. They, too, were in a slump, but Stein recognised that the Edinburgh

McNeill's immediate precursor as organiser of Celtic's defence, Bobby Evans had 385 games for Celtic from 1945 until his transfer to Chelsea in 1960.

club had more potential – and there was probably little more he could do for Dunfermline.

He was there only eight months. He started by winning the Summer Cup, a minor competition which used to fill up those empty months when the rest of Britain transferred its sporting allegiances to cricket. He brought over the great Real Madrid side to Easter Road for a friendly and beat them 2-0 in front of a 32,000 crowd. He put Hibs into a potentially Championship-winning position when the club beat Rangers in Edinburgh in front of 44,000. Then, on 1 February and out of the blue, it was announced that he would be taking up the job as Celtic's new manager.

In view of what Stein was to achieve, the move seemed logical and sensible. In fact, he was taking over a club which had fallen on distinctly hard times and which, throughout the early part of the Sixties, had mounted no real challenge to a Rangers side containing such fine players as Ian McMillan, Jimmy Millar, Ralph Brand and the sublime Jim Baxter.

Statistically, their post-War record was pathetic. In the 20 years since 1945, Celtic had won the League only once and the Scottish Cup and the League Cup twice. They had talented players like Bobby Evans and Bobby Collins, but both had been allowed to leave. Chairman Robert Kelly ruled the club with a rod of iron and manager Jimmy McGrory had to accept that he was not always master of his own house.

This was no bad background for an aspiring manager. Stein had done all he could for Dunfermline and possibly Hibs, but he realised that reviving Celtic was not only a bigger job but the potential for improvement dramatically increased. He may have had no idea what a phenomenal reign he was to have at Parkhead – but he was certain that his own philosophy of the game would be sufficient to get the club off the floor.

What he did was to instill organisation, attention to detail and a willingness to work. He did so a group of young players who were prepared to listen, many of whom had just been starting their careers when Stein was previously with the club as reserve team manager. Like Shankly

Jock Stein at his desk at Parkhead.

and Busby, Stein did not believe that there were any secrets in being a successful manager, but he knew that football rewarded those who were prepared to work at it. No-one worked harder than Stein.

His first match in charge of the club was at Airdrie, where Celtic won 6-0. Tommy Gemmell, who was to become a Lisbon Lion, remembers it well. It says much about the new man's approach. 'We were all desperately keen to impress him. I had a reputation of being an overlapping full-back and that night I never stopped. I was up and down that field until I was ready to drop and had a hand in a couple of goals. When we came into the dressing room at the finish I thought I had done enough to get a pat on the back. Instead Mr Stein said to me: ''Well played - but don't forget you are a full-back first.'''

Bobby Murdoch, powerful midfield creator with a tremendous shot, in action in the 1970 League Cup final against Rangers.

Above *Goal-scoring winger Bobby Lennox played 296 League games for Celtic between 1962 and 1980, a key member of the most successful squad in the club's history.*

Below *Definitive exponent of the Scottish winger's art, Jimmy Johnstone delighted in tying opposing defences in knots.*

He always gave them good value, right from the start. He arrived at Celtic Park on 9 March 1965. He called the players around him and said : 'I promise to do the best for you, but in return you must do your best for me.' Just six weeks later he was guiding Celtic out at Hampden Park in a Scottish Cup Final against his old club Dumfermline.

There was an interesting preamble to the game. Celtic had never quite accepted that the manager was totally, utterly, completely in control of team matters. Stein's predecessor was the immensely likeable McGrory, who had led the club through good times and bad. But the real power lay with the chairman Robert Kelly.

Of all the many aspects of the club which changed under Stein's rule, probably the most important was the fact that, from now on, the manager managed. When, two days before the final, Stein showed Kelly the team list, the chairman was unconvinced that Bobby Murdoch was the right man at wing half. 'Well,' answered Stein, 'on Saturday you will find out that he is.'

In later years, the picture of the first of his Cup-winning teams was the largest photograph displayed in his tiny office. It reminded him of a day when Dunfermline took the lead, Bertie Auld equalized and finally Billy McNeill headed the winner.

That Cup win was just a glorious overture for 10 years of uninterrupted success, the like of which Scottish football had never seen before. Celtic, indeed, were almost too successful. Others, even Rangers, began to think of them as unstoppable. While one club carried all before them, the others slumped. Gates were down. It needed the introduction of the 10-club Premier League in the mid-seventies to revive football's fortunes. But you could hardly blame Celtic for being head and shoulders above the opposition.

The Cup had to be followed by the League . . . and it duly was in the 1965–66 season. Celtic served notice of their intentions by beating Rangers to win the League Cup in October. John Hughes, that gifted, erratic and crowd-pleasing winger, scored both goals. But there was crowd trouble at the finish when Rangers fans tried to interrupt Celtic's lap of honour – and the result was that this kind of celebration was banned for the next few years.

Stein hated the hooliganism which at this time was a distinct problem for football. He hated it as much amongst his own fans as amongst the supporters of Celtic's rivals. On more than one occasion he went on to terraces to add his own considerable weight to that of the police. 'We don't want them. They are not football people,' he would say with feeling. He disliked intensely anything which took the dignity out of a game which supplied him with his living.

It was a curious League season. When the Old Firm met at Parkhead in front of 66,000 fans for the traditional New Year game, they were level on points. But Steve Chalmers scored three goals in a 5-1 win and it looked as if the club would now make a steady progress towards the title.

But it did not work that way. By March Rangers were in the lead by two points. Celtic had undergone a troublesome experience in trying to play their European Cup-Winners' Cup-tie against Dynamo Kiev. The Russians switched the tie to Tbilisi in Georgia to escape rough winter weather. A combination of mechanical failures and unscheduled stops made the return journey take 48 hours, rubbing the gloss off a 1-1 draw. It left Celtic too tired and miserable for anything other than a defeat at Tynecastle by Hearts on the Saturday to again leave Rangers in the lead.

In fact Celtic were to go out of the Cup-Winners' Cup in the semi-final to Liverpool and lose the Scottish Cup Final to Rangers before eventually claiming the Championship by the narrowest of margins at Motherwell.

Stein's charges had just about managed to fall over the finishing line intact.

Stein had made his authority tell in a number of ways. He had gained the players' interest by improving the training routines. Lapping the track day after day was no old-fashioned phenomenon in the Sixties. Stein made sure that all work was done with the ball. He had firmly convinced the side that he was a players' man. And he was already tinkering with the make-up of the club.

He was always a great believer in 'creative tension.' That meant that players performed best when the places were kept challenged by reserves. This was never more obvious than at the start of the Seventies when Davie

Tommy Gemmell heads the ball out of defence in a 1970 League match against Hearts. He was one of the earliest and best overlapping backs in the British game.

Tommy Callaghan was one of the post-Lisbon Lions generation, Stein securing him from Dunfermline before the 1968–9 season.

May, Danny McGrain, George Connelly, Kenny Dalglish and Lou Macari were all patiently waiting to move up to first-team football.

The manager had signed Ronnie Simpson from Hibs to replace John Fallon as the recognised first team goalkeeper. Jim Craig arrived from, of all places, Glasgow University. In February of the Championship year, Stein made a crucial switch, bringing in Bertie Auld as Murdoch's regular partner in midfield. He added Joe McBride to the striking force, buying him from Motherwell for £20,000. Briefly, until injury dictated otherwise, McBride was the greatest scorer in the country.

For the players, it really was like living in a new era. Despite his dislike of jargon, Stein was not averse to bringing out the blackboard to make a point. Opposing teams were analysed, although he always much preferred to stress Celtic's strengths. Individuals were given specific jobs to do. If they completed them properly, the overall teamwork would look after itself. The manager never asked a player to do something foreign to his natural game. Above all, he was fiercely defensive of his squad, shielding them from outside criticism. In the dressing room, he found a responsive audience.

But no-one could really have anticipated 1967, which was to be the annus mirabilis, the greatest season enjoyed by any club in the history of British football. Every trophy up for grabs ended at Celtic Park. At the end of the season, when Liverpool's manager, Bill Shankly, strode into the Lisbon dressing room at the end of the European Cup Final, he said only two words to Stein. They are now part of the game's history – but looking back, it is hard to think he could have said anything else. Grasping Stein like a long-lost brother, all he said was 'You're immortal.'

Stein said later that the seeds of Scottish and European success was sown in North America, where they played pre-season friendlies against Spurs and Bayern Munich amongst others. There was something in this, because the manager had always believed in the value of being 'on the road.'

When they went into Europe, Celtic frequently travelled on a Monday morning and returned Thursday afternoon. The modern practice is to make these trips as short as possible, but Stein liked to study his players closely away from the inevitable distractions of Glasgow. Under his management there was no skimping either. Any member of the Lisbon Lions could boast that he had stayed in many of Europe's best five-star hotels.

There were never any disciplinary problems. One of the many astonishing aspects of this remarkable man was that he seemed to exist on very little sleep. After dinner – he was a sturdy eater – Stein would normally take up position in the foyer, watching the world go by, talking to officials and pressmen and drinking endless cups of tea. If the players had been out for the evening, there was no way to bed except by walking past the manager. And, as a life long teetotaller, he could smell drink a mile away.

The greatest of all seasons saw the first piece of silverware safely harvested by the end of October when Celtic retained the League Cup, again beating Rangers in the Final. Bobby Lennox scored the winning goal from a long Auld cross and a carefully measured header by McBride.

Stein had one lucky break as winter drew on. He decided that he needed another striker and went out and bought Willie Wallace from Hearts. He did not know it but McBride, then the leading scorer, was soon to be hampered by injury and would be unable to play his fullest part in the campaigns.

In the League, Celtic had one bogey team, Dundee United, who managed to beat them twice, but Rangers were beaten early on and eventually a 2-2 draw at Ibrox, both goals from Jimmy Johnstone, took them to the title. In the Scottish Cup Final, Wallace proved what a shrewd signing he had been when he scored both goals against Aberdeen. With the minor Glasgow Cup already won, it only remained for the European Cup to come to Parkhead and there would be an East End celebration that would put VE night into the shade.

Stein had always accepted that Scotland was a small country and the only real way to improve standards was to measure yourself against the best of other nations. He had never accepted the parochialism which had left Scots unquestioningly believing, against all evidence, that they were the best football people in the world. He had admired Hungary with Puskás, had thrilled to Real Madrid and Di Stéfano and had been to see Helenio Herrera,

Harry Hood arrived at Parkhead from Clyde; like Callaghan, he earned his first winner's medal in the 1969 League Cup final.

that master of Italian defence, now the manager of Inter Milan.

In the preliminary round, Celtic had a comfortable victory over Zürich, winning 2-0 at Parkhead and 3-0 in the away leg. In the first round proper they were equally impressive, seeing off Nantes 3-1 home and away for a 6-2 aggregate margin. For the quarter finals, Celtic were presented with the rugged Vojvodina of Yugoslavia, against whom they struggled to go down 0-1 in the first away leg. The return was going to be difficult because not only was McBride still injured but Wallace was ineligible. It was going to be one of those nights of patient play, a long hard stint at breaking down a stubborn defence. By half-time, Celtic had not made a dent but after 60 minutes, the Voyvodina goalkeeper fumbled the ball and Steve Chalmers swept it into the net.

Time was running out. But McNeill, as he had done in the Scottish Cup Final two years before, was a captain capable of rising to the occasion. His header put Celtic into the last four, and Parkhead had never known quite such an emotional occasion.

The semi-final, against mighty Dukla Prague, represented Stein with a dilemma. Willie Wallace had scored two goals as Celtic won 3-1 in Glasgow but the manager was not convinced that this was anything like a match-winning lead. The club had thrown away a bigger advantage in the 1964 Cup-Winners' Cup-tie against MTK of Budapest. For a man for whom attack was a moral crusade, Stein succumbed to the biggest challenge to that philosophy and sadly sent Celtic out to defend. Only Steve Chalmers was left up front and, indeed, the goalless draw was exactly what Celtic wanted. But the manager looked strained and unhappy. 'We'll never do that again,' he said afterwards.

It all meant that Celtic were in the final against the aristocrats of Italy, Inter Milan, and for the first time a side composed completely of local players were about to make their mark on the biggest competition in club football. History was in the making.

That history was written in Lisbon on 25 May 1967 by goals from Tommy Gemmell and Steve Chalmers. Part of Stein's image was that of a man who can keep his head while others were losing theirs. He always seemed unruffled. But as the final seconds of the final ticked away, he could bear it no longer. Stein rose from the bench and headed for the dressing rooms, only for the final whistle to sound as he was walking down to the touchline. He embraced Ronnie Simpson first.

In the days leading up to the match, though, he grew in stature. In every interview, he stressed that the performance of the fans was as important as that of the players. He kept on contrasting Inter's defensive tactics, as opposed to Celtic's emphasis on attack. It was all designed to grab hold of the Portugese support. A master propagandist, Stein never missed a trick.

In training sessions, he simulated Inter's style of play and plotted means of breaking it down. In Lisbon, he told his players to keep out of the sun and deliberately arranged a training session in early evening at exactly the same time as the the real kick-off. He could not believe it when, entering the stadium before the match, he saw thousands upon thousands of Celtic supporters. It remained a mystery to him throughout his career just how the fans could afford to make the trips and buy the tickets.

It all went right in the final. Celtic attacked, deeply and overwhelmingly, and eventually Inter caved in not only to the sustained pressure but also to the great belief that Celtic had in themselves. Stein had given the side a confidence which was worth an extra man. Billy McNeill took the massive trophy, the fans swamped the pitch and Stein sat quietly in the dressing room, muttering over and over again 'What a performance, what a performance.' No-one was arguing with him.

Bertie Auld was jumping up and down shouting : 'What are we ? We are the Greatest — that's what we are.' Later on Auld asked Stein, 'Do you think anyone will ever beat us ?' 'No,' said Stein, 'No one will ever beat that team.' The reply was thoughtfully made and indeed the side which won the European Cup never made another appearance again in competitive football. It was part of the man's notion of protecting those idols that he would not allow some other side to say later: 'We beat the Lisbon Lions.' He wasn't going to give anyone a chance. More seriously, he wondered to himself : 'What will they want next?'

If the claiming of the European Cup in 1967 was the pinnacle of Stein's career, the nine successive Championships were its backbone. The man had plenty of qualities – an awesome personality which commanded respect, an unfailing attention to detail – but above all he retained an enthusiasm very rarely tainted with cynicism. He made people see things his way, manipulating the media, encouraging players and above all taking care of supporters.

His was an uncomplicated theory of management. At a time when a new breed of coaches, influenced by the way Alf Ramsey had won the World Cup for England in 1966, were introducing the jargon of technology into the game, he would have none of it. The other half of his 'secret' was that he would never ask a player to do a job which was outside his capabilities. He could isolate a talent and then fit it into the side.

All those abilities went into making Celtic a consistent team. In those nine years of almost unfaltering triumph, there was a calm certainty about his decisions and they mostly worked. Just occasionally he underestimated the opposition, as when Partick Thistle beat Celtic 4-1 in the 1971 Scottish League Cup Final; but those aberrations were few and far between.

He expected his men to work hard. At the root of this was the belief that the supporters deserved no less than complete effort from their team. 'They don't have a lot to cheer about in life. Watching Celtic costs them money that maybe they can't afford. So we must never short-change them.' Although a complete football person through and through, he never forgot that the game's most important people are those who stand on the terraces.

George Connelly shoots past Leeds United keeper Gary Sprake in the first minute of the first leg of the epic 1970 European Cup semi-final.

What Stein gave them, of course, was seven more Championships plus assorted Scottish and League Cups and another European Cup final. But in a sense he was right. There could never be another season like it. He was at the height of his power and at the height of his fame. The Lisbon win achieved a lot of things, not least placing Stein amongst the coterie of truly great managers alongside Chapman, Shankly and Busby. Stein remained a football person, turning down many offers from outside the game which could have made him rich. He could never stay away from the ground for long. In early Celtic days there had been a tradition that on Sunday, the dressing rooms should be opened up, the boiler turned on and the local population could come in for free baths. That had long been abandoned but most Sunday mornings Stein would hold court to assembled friends, the occasional player, passing supporters and the Press.

He would analyse the previous day's matches. He would offer his views on the international scene. In those ways, he controlled a great deal of what was written about football, not just about Celtic's football. He was a great manipulator of men.

His judgment in the transfer market stayed sound. By the 1968-69 season he had bought Tom Callaghan from Dunfermline and Harry Hood from Clyde. He was later to sign Dixie Deans from Motherwell, another shrewd move. And he also had that amazing bunch of young players – nicknamed The Quality Street Gang – ready to press their claims. The club was in very capable hands, and able to withstand such setbacks as a quick exit to Dynamo Kiev in the very first defence of the European Cup, the World Club Cup Championship debacle against Racing Club, and the loss of the 1970 European Cup final to Feyenoord.

The successes more than made up for that. In the semi-final of the 1969–70 European Cup, Celtic established an all-time record for that competition when 134,000 turned out for the second leg against Leeds United at Hampden Park. The goals from Hughes and Murdoch that evening were a special joy as Celtic won 2-1. Stein had always thought that his club's achievements were recognised everywhere apart from England.

The same could also be said for his own achievements. Many would argue, with justification, that it will always be one of life's injustices that Stein wasn't Scotland's first soccer knight in the same way that Sir Matt Busby was honoured for Manchester United's European Cup triumph the following season.

Victory over Leeds was, in many ways, Celtic's Last Hurrah. The defeat in the final against Feyenoord broke the magical spell which had persisted since 1965. Celtic, for the first time under Stein, had been branded as complacent in their attitude to a team which was heralding a new period of Dutch supremacy in European football. Celtic did force extra time before Kindvall decided the issue.

The Championships kept rolling in – but the European results, Stein's barometer of the club's health – were sometimes disappointing. A major blow to his morale came in 1972 when Celtic reached the European Cup semi-final, meeting once again those old foes from Inter Milan. Celtic defended in Milan, Inter did the same in Glasgow, even through extra time, and it went to penalty deciders. Deans promptly missed the spot kick and Celtic were out in the most harrowing way of all.

'We may have a better team in years ahead but who can say we will ever have a better chance of winning the European Cup?' Stein said.

That possibility started to disappear in the following season as three of the most gifted young players – Macari, Dalglish and Hay – were all transferred to England while a fourth, the immensely talented George Connelly, dropped out of football altogether. Some of the replacements were more than adequate buys. Johnny Doyle, later tragically killed, became a firm favourite with the fans and Johannes Edvaldsson was a big strong Icelander, comfortable in a variety of positions.

Again in 1974, Celtic reached the semi-finals of the European Cup, a fact which shows that if during the Seventies they were in slow decline, then they were at least descending from heights to which no other Scottish club had ever climbed. The match against Atlético Madrid at Parkhead could only have soured Stein. Three Atlético players were sent off and seven booked as they deliberately sent out a shadow side of expendable players to disrupt the tie. Their manager was Juan Carlos Lorenzo, who had been in charge of the Argentina national team beaten by England in the quarter finals of the 1966 World Cup.

Below *Kenny Dalglish creates havoc in the Dundee United defence in the 1974 Scottish Cup final.*

After a goal-less draw in the home leg, Stein kept his players quartered in a Madrid hotel. They scarcely trained, received a death threat against Jimmy Johnstone and were secretly quite relieved that they escaped intact, even though losing the tie 0-2.

The stress was telling on Stein. A workaholic, he had spent long hours at Parkhead, had never wasted an opportunity to motor down to England where, it was joked, he had a season ticket at Manchester United (he had turned down an offer to manage the club in 1970), and was setting impossibly high standards. He did not quite share with the later teams the affinity he had held with his Lisbon Lions. Contract disputes hurt him and the big deals looked for by younger players who had scarcely served their apprenticeship all saddened him. He would still be fierce, occasionally with referees, but he looked like a man beginning to feel that he had done all he could for the club. Fate was about to deal him a cruel hand.

Stein was returning home from a holiday in Minorca in July 1975 along with his wife Jean, Bob Shankly (Bill's brother) and his wife Margaret, and his long-time pal, bookmaker Tony Queen. Near Lockerbie on the notorious A74, he was in collision with a Peugeot which was travelling on the wrong side of the carriageway.

In a head-on crash, the two women were not badly hurt and neither was Shankly. But Stein and his friend took the brunt and were immediately rushed to the Dumfries Royal Infirmary.

Stein underwent an emergency operation to relieve his breathing and his miner's constitution eventually carried him to a complete recovery, although those close to him believe that it was that crash which not only mellowed him but cut back his insatiable desire to put football above all other things in life.

Stein was a month in hospital, receiving no visitors apart from his immediate family, before he was allowed to go home. 'He will return to Celtic in his own good time, whenever he feels like it, after whatever period of convalescence he needs,' said Celtic chairman Desmond White.

In a curious way, Stein's influence at Parkhead was best illustrated by what happened when he was not there. Although he had been to a reserve match in August, it was quite clear that his health would not permit him any active running of the club. It was an important season because the Premier League – the new streamlined top 10 in Scottish football – was in operation for the first time and Stein had set his sights on it.

Celtic fell by the wayside. They lost the autumn League Cup final by a single goal to Rangers and Motherwell put them out of the Scottish Cup, having come back from two goals down. It is impossible to conclude anything but the fact that, without 'The Big Man' at the helm, Celtic's ship was beached.

Thirteen months after the accident Stein returned to the club and appointed Dave McParland, the man who had led Thistle to that League Cup win, as his assistant. He quickly made a major signing, Pat Stanton from Hibs. He surprised everybody by buying former Rangers player Alfie Conn from Spurs and Conn became the first player in over half a century to play for both halves of the Old Firm.

That was pure showmanship, but the two new men, along with Joe Craig, an effective centre forward from Partick Thistle, helped to create a new chapter in the Stein legend. For the sixth time in 12 years Celtic won the League and Cup double, which climaxed when an Andy Lynch penalty beat Rangers in the final. Although the club went out of the UEFA Cup in the first round to Wisla Krakow, it was considered a highly successful season – and proof that the Stein personality was still at work.

Johannes Edvaldsson, the sturdy Icelander, was a useful utility player in the mid-1970s and won a Scottish Cup-winners' medal in 1977.

It was, however, just a parting shot from Stein as a club manager. Season 1977-78 was a disaster. Celtic reached the League Cup final, only to be beaten by Rangers. They were knocked out of the Cup by First Division Kilmarnock and finished only fifth in the Premier League.

The reason was not hard to find. Celtic had been signing players far inferior to those who had launched the Stein era. Many of the best young prospects had been allowed, for various reasons, to go. The quality was lacking at Parkhead and the club seemed reluctant to spend after all the years of glorious success – but quite suddenly at the end of the season Stein was gone. Billy McNeill was appointed the new manager, the old captain replacing the King.

It is still not clear whether he jumped or whether he was pushed. Chairman White said 'No matter how talented and successful a manager, the time comes when the pressures and the strains start to take their toll. As well as knowing better than most just what those pressures are, Jock Stein suffered severe physical injury as the innocent victim of a major car accident. Those factors combined to bring home to him several months ago that the time was opportune for the directors to consider seriously the question of a successor.'

Stein was offered a place on the board and a job developing Celtic's commercial activities. It was not to his liking. After a testimonial match against Liverpool (and Dalglish) which grossed £80,000 from a 60,000 crowd, he was quite suddenly out of football – but not for long.

He went to Leeds United, but for only seven weeks, or, to be totally accurate 45 days. Then, when Scotland manager Ally McLeod was dismissed in the lingering trauma of the World Cup fiasco in Argentina in 1978, Stein decided to accept the challenge. He left Leeds as quickly as he had arrived – to start on a second career of bringing his authority to bear on a whole country, rather than on a single club.

Stein was uniquely fitted for this role. Indeed every time the job had come up in the previous 15 years, his name was inevitably linked with it. But it had gone in turn to Tommy Docherty, Willie Ormond, and then the unfortunate McLeod.

After adequate Scotland performances in the 1982 World Cup in Spain, Stein embarked on the qualifying matches for Mexico '86. In a close group, it all came down to Scotland's last match against Wales at Cardiff on 10 September 1985. Wales were difficult opponents. They had opened up the group by beating Scotland at Hampden through a goal of stunning virtuosity by Ian Rush. Stein needed a draw in Wales, and that looked unlikely when Scotland went behind to a first half goal. But substitute Davie Cooper transformed the situation in the second half and scored an equalizing (if extremely dubious) penalty. Mexico seemed to beckon.

Stein looked pinched and drawn. There had been some ill-feeling between the two dug-outs. Suddenly he collapsed and was helped down into the tunnel by the team's doctor, Stuart Hillis, a heart specialist. He died there. 'There was nothing we could do, and the tragedy was that all the equipment was there to help him. We couldn't revive him.'

The last words Stein uttered were to the same doctor. As the match entered its last seconds, he said: 'Whatever happens, we must not lose our dignity.' That was his epitaph. Another was spoken by one of a group of stunned Scots who gathered outside Ninian Park and watched in silence, their celebrations having turned to deep grief.

'I'll tell you something,' he said, 'I wish we weren't going to Mexico and that man was still alive.'

Alfie Conn, who came to Celtic from Tottenham in 1977, was the first player to earn Scottish Cup-winners' medals with both Rangers (1973) and Celtic (1977). What's more, both these finals were Auld Firm affairs.

47

McNeill the Manager

Preceding pages *Skipper
Danny McGrain, one of the finest
backs in Britain in the 1970s and
early 1980s, holds the 1982
Premier League championship
trophy aloft.*

Billy McNeill was the obvious choice as Jock Stein's successor as manager of
Celtic. Indeed, it looked as if he had been groomed for that role for some
years. After bowing out with the Scottish Cup in his hands in 1975, he had
gone to Clyde to serve his apprenticeship. The small club, which always had
close links with Celtic, prospered under his management. He discovered a
young forward called Steve Archibald, whom he was to take to Aberdeen
and eventually sell to Spurs for £800,000.

He then succeeded Ally McCleod in the Granite City as Scottish football's
big talker took up the Scotland job that was to end so disastrously in
Argentina. There he bought Gordon Strachan from Dundee, launched the
careers of Willie Miller and Jim Leighton, and laid some of the foundation
stones that helped Alex Ferguson take the club to all the Scottish trophies –
and the European Cup-Winners' Cup. McNeill was obviously the manager
in waiting.

It was not altogether an easy decision for McNeill to return. His family
enjoyed Aberdeen, where football was put in its context, not unimportant
but certainly not a matter of life and death. He could sense that the best of
Aberdeen was still to come, while Celtic were down in the dumps. In the
end, though, there was no real decision to make. McNeill had always been
Celtic through and through.

When McNeill took over, on the eve of that World Cup in 1978, Celtic had
endured a painful season. They finished only fifth in the League, for the first
time in 29 years they had been put out of the Cup by a lower division side,

*Billy McNeill in 1987 at the
start of his first triumphant
season in his second spell as
Parkhead supremo.*

they had lost to Rangers in the final of the League Cup and staggered out of Europe, beaten by the Austrians of SW Innsbruck.

The new manager was clear what was wrong: 'It has become obvious that some players do not deserve to be wearing Celtic jerseys. Too few of them seem to realise what playing for a club like ours means'.

'You have to be prepared to work and sacrifice and play until you drop. We are an extraordinary club and we demand extraordinary standards.' His immediate task was to strengthen his squad and his first two purchases were clever and successful. Davie Provan, an exciting winger, arrived from Kilmarnock. Murdo MacLeod, a workhorse midfielder, arrived from Dumbarton. They cost between them £220,000 – and in the seasons to come were worth every penny. A more exciting, even quixotic signing was the recall of Bobby Lennox, then playing in the United States with Houston Hurricanes. He had lost none of his legendary enthusiasm, and little of his pace either.

McNeill's baptism was not immediately successful. For the first time in 14 years the club did not reach the Final of the League Cup, losing to Rangers in a bitter semi which ended up with a player from each side being sent off before an own goal gave the Ibrox club an extra-time victory.

But the long haul in the League gave them a better chance and the Championship race turned out to be as exciting as any in history. After a long hard winter, Celtic found themselves in the bottom half of the table, owing largely to the number of games which had been postponed. But with Danny McGrain returning to the side as skipper after an absence of 18 months, the charge was on.

Murdo MacLeod, a skilful, industrious midfielder, played 237 matches between his arrival from Dumbarton in 1980 and his departure to Borussia Dortmund in 1987.

It looked to have been a brave but futile effort when Rangers beat them 1-0 to take a one-point lead with only four games left. But over the last few games, Celtic went unbeaten – and victory for them, again over Rangers, in their very final match at Parkhead would give them the title. Seldom has even an Old Firm game ever been as crucial.

It was, by any standards, an extraordinary game. After 55 minutes, Rangers not only led by one goal but Celtic winger Johnny Doyle had been sent off. What was then to happen started the legend that Celtic were always at their most dangerous when reduced to ten men. With a draw suiting Rangers, it looked all over. Then, Roy Aitken scored the equaliser and George McCluskey put his side ahead. Parkhead was in bedlam but that was silenced when 13 minutes from the end Bobby Russell made it 2-2. The equation was simple. Celtic had to score again to win the League.

They did more than that. They took the lead when a McCluskey cross was palmed out only to hit Colin Jackson and spin into the net off the centre half's leg. And it was embellished when MacLeod hit a memorable 20-yard drive to make it 4-2. McNeill had savoured his first taste of success at the club.

But it was not all plain-sailing in the season that followed, largely because Aberdeen were confirming the promise that McNeill knew they had. Not only that, but Jim McLean's patience at Tannadice was paying off. The New Firm won the League and the League Cup, leaving Celtic to concentrate on the Scottish Cup. They reached the final against Rangers, largely with the side from the previous season but also with Frank McGarvey, bought from Liverpool, where he had never settled, for £250,000.

It was a good final, but one remembered for the wrong reasons. The game was settled in extra time when McGrain's shot was deflected by McCluskey out of goalkeeper McCloy's reach. That was enough to re-confirm Celtic as Scotland's best Cup fighters, but the scenes at the end of the match soured the triumph. Celtic took the Cup towards their end of Hampden Park and the

Busy, combative striker Frank McGarvey broke the Scottish transfer record with his £250,000 move from Liverpool in 1980 and soon formed a productive partnership with Charlie Nicholas. He joined St Mirren in 1985, gaining a Cup-winner's medal with them in 1987.

supporters came out of the terraces to join in the celebrations. Rangers fans invaded the pitch at the other end of the ground and a battle was inevitable. It was quelled only by the use of mounted police – and the pictures went all round the world.

Both clubs were fined £20,000 – but the long-term effect was greater, and for the good. The resulting Criminal Justice (Scotland) Act followed which banned alcohol from grounds and from the buses taking fans to games. Towards the end of the Eighties, Scotland could congratulate itself on its efforts to eradicate the hooligan problem, a direct legacy of that final. But it was a shame that the innocent celebrations of the Celtic supporters had set those wheels in motion.

McNeill was now firmly in charge. Rangers, by their standards, were struggling and Scottish football was facing an exciting time with the traditional Old Firm supremacy under threat by the two clubs in the North East. The outcome of that challenge was good for Scottish football. There was no room for complacency.

Celtic won the Championship again in 1981, the season in which Charlie Nicholas burst into the side to form a potent striking partnership with McGarvey, who became the country's leading goalscorer. When the title was won at Tannadice, Celtic could afford to prean themselves. They had won the Premier League with the most points scored, the most wins and the most goals.

They won it again the next season, as Paul McStay became the latest talented youngster to break through into the top team. This was a particularly satisfying win because Aberdeen, who lost only one of their last 20 matches, were at their height and Celtic had to battle all the way. It seemed to suit them. On the last day of the League, Celtic knew that if they lost 1-0 at home to St Mirren and Aberdeen could beat Rangers 5-0 at Pittodrie, the title would go to the Granite City. The scenario seemed unlikely but at one stage the Dons led 4-0 and at the same time Celtic were being held 0-0. Celtic eventually scored in the 63rd minute through McCluskey and that set a 40,000 crowd singing as Tom McAdam and McCluskey again scored. At a time when Celtic seemed to win most of their titles on other people's grounds, the celebrations were loud and long. Threequarters of an hour after the match, the crowds were still on the terraces, shouting the name of Johnny Doyle, the popular winger who had tragically electrocuted himself in his house earlier in the season. There were a few players who wept for him.

After a poor period in the Cup competitions, Celtic beat Rangers in the 1982 League Cup final to win that trophy for the first time in eight years. The cheekiness of Nicholas's opening goal was matched by the power of MacLeod's later effort.

There was one other fine effort that season when Ajax of Amsterdam were beaten in the European Cup. Celtic could manage only a 2-2 draw against the Dutchmen, Cruyff included, in front of 56,000 at Parkhead in the first leg. But somehow they held on in the second and McCluskey's late goal gave them a 2-1 win to take the tie in Amsterdam. It was a performance reminiscent of the great European nights. Sadly, Real Sociedad put them out in the next round.

They took the League to the last day, on which three clubs could win. Dundee United led by a point from Aberdeen and Celtic.

On an afternoon when a transistor was the most vital piece of equipment on the terraces, United held on and the fact that Celtic had overturned a two-goal deficit at Ibrox against Rangers to win 4-2 didn't matter. Few could have believed that this was to be McNeill's last competitive game in charge.

The manager had brought back consistency and determination to the club. As he said when he took over, the place demanded extraordinary standards and these had been applied. McNeill was a players' manager, just as long as a player gave everything he had for the club. In his first period as manager, he had cultivated the usual crop of good Celtic youngsters, like McStay and Nicholas, while buying in the transfer market at fees which were never inflated.

It seemed that, in the aftermath of Stein, the sense of tradition and continuity which had always been important to the club, had been re-established. The fans thought that the challenge of the New Firm would go away. Rangers were still far short of showing all their potential. Quite suddenly, all that was thrown into confusion.

McNeill started the 1983 season, business as usual. He had bowed to the inevitable and transferred Charlie Nicholas to Arsenal for £750,000. As Nicholas went, the replacement arrived: Brian McClair from Motherwell, for a tenth of that price. Four years later, he too would go – to Manchester United for £800,000.

At the same time McNeill was arguing privately with the Celtic directors that his salary should be increased. The matter became public and the wrangling somewhat acrimonious. Facing McNeill was the club chairman Desmond White, then in his seventies. Relationships between the two men had never been cordial. McNeill resented the fact that while he was negotiating salary increases for the players, nothing was done about his own position.

Eventually, it was Manchester City which decided the situation. Just relegated to the Second Division, they saw McNeill as an obvious choice to lead them back to the First. McNeill left.

Brian McClair, a brilliant replacement for Charlie Nicholas, led the Premier League with 23 goals in his first Celtic season, 1983–4. In 1987 Alex Ferguson lured him south to Old Trafford.

Charlie Nicholas, one of the great Parkhead cult figures, won a championship medal in 1981 and led the League with 29 goals in 1983. He then spent four and a half largely fruitless years with Arsenal before joining Aberdeen at the end of 1987.

Pat Bonner, Celtic's first choice between the sticks since 1980, is now a crucial member of Eire's international side. He played superbly in the Republic's remarkable performances in the 1988 European Championship.

Celtic Centenary Season 1987–8

When Roy Aitken finally laid his hands on the gleaming Scottish League trophy, the 44,000 Parkhead crowd cheered and broke into song. But instead of the usual anthem, they belted out 'Happy Birthday!' More than anything else, Celtic wanted to celebrate their centenary with the Championship. They had done it – and on the League season's last Saturday, they held the silverware high.

It was their 35th Championship in those 100 years. They had established a new points total which, when the Premier League reverts to 10 clubs, will never be beaten. In his office, manager Billy McNeill was revealing some other statistics behind the triumph. It was the largest winning margin in the history of the Premier League. With only three games lost, it was the least of any of the previous winners. And in 28 out of 44 games, Celtic's opponents had failed to score against them.

It was, quite simply, a triumph as rich as it was unexpected. Exactly 12 months before Celtic had been jeered off the same pitch, losing their last match of the season to Falkirk, who needed the points to stay up. Fans had disgustedly thrown their scarves at manager Davie Hay. And, as it entered its 100th year, the old club seemed to be in disarray. To turn the place around – and counter the champions Rangers who had spent over £6,000,000 in the two-year reign of Graeme Souness – was as good a fairy story as Scottish football has permitted in this century.

Fate played its part. Within weeks of that last disastrous match, McNeill was getting the sack from Aston Villa. The man who had brought home the European Cup in 1967 had gone to England after falling out with Celtic five years earlier over his salary. He had managed Manchester City, then gone to Villa; but as the club slumped into the Second Division, he was fired. It was a traumatic moment for a 46-year-old who had known only success during his 30 years in the game.

Ironically, McNeill was due back in Glasgow for a 20th reunion of the Lisbon Lions and he was to be out of work for less than three weeks. On 27 May he was invited to an unusual meeting. Calling on the telephone was Celtic chairman Jack McGinn. Would McNeill meet him in a car park in Clydebank.? There could be only one reason for the rendezvous. Later, the new manager said that it had taken him 'less than one second' to agree to come back, like a prodigal son, to the only club where he had ever truly belonged.

The next day, McGinn informed Hay that his services were no longer needed. That was a pity for a man who was universally liked. He could take some solace from the general suggestion that he was too nice a guy for the profession of football manager. But on 28 May McNeill walked into a press conference held at Celtic Park. 'It was like winning the European Cup, the pools and the Derby on the same day,' he said.

The new man took over a club in some turmoil. Mo Johnston, Brian McClair, Alan McInally and Murdo MacLeod had already said that they wished to exercise their rights under freedom of contract and were all about to sign for other clubs – Nantes, Manchester United, Aston Villa and Borussia Dortmund respectively. Although Hay had signed defender Mick McCarthy from Manchester City for £500,000, the Parkhead cupboard looked ominously bare.

McNeill knew he could rely on a backbone of senior professionals like Pat Bonner, Paul McStay, Roy Aitken and Tommy Burns; but he was acutely aware that he needed goalscorers. It was to be his skill in the transfer market during the coming weeks which would put Celtic en route to the title.

McNeill made three major signings – Frank McAvennie, Joe Miller and Andy Walker – during the summer and autumn, but backed those up with two more which confirmed his reputation as a shrewd assessor of talent. Billy Stark arrived from Aberdeen for £75,000 and Chris Morris was acquired from Sheffield Wednesday for £100,000. They proved to be just as vital pieces of the jigsaw he was putting together.

Walker was the first of the big names to come to Parkhead. With every other club in Scotland knowing that Celtic were desperate to replace their lost strikers – and recognising also that they must have close on £2,000,000 in the bank – McNeill had to pay what appeared to be an inflated price to get the young, obviously talented but essentially unproven Walker from

Motherwell. His end-of-season tally of 31 goals proved that he was a bargain.

As a partner for Walker, McNeill instinctively thought about Charlie Nicholas, who was finding it difficult to get a game for Arsenal. The two men were friends and the Parkhead crowd had been chanting his name and increasing the pressure for the return of one prodigal son to be followed by another. McNeill inquired of Arsenal manager George Graham; but Nicholas decided to stay in England. Then half way through the season he went north to Aberdeen, so that signing must go under the heading of what might have been.

Instead, McNeill decided that Frank McAvennie's strength and pace would be ideal foils for Walker's poaching. At first West Ham United were

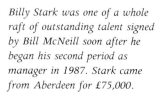

Billy Stark was one of a whole raft of outstanding talent signed by Bill McNeill soon after he began his second period as manager in 1987. Stark came from Aberdeen for £75,000.

insisting that it would take £1,500,000 to prize him away from Upton Park. That sort of money was out of the question; but McNeill was nothing if not persistant. Dozens of phone calls later, he had worn down the resolve of the London club and £850,000 brought McAvennie to the place where he had stood on the terraces as a kid. He soon shed a lot of weight, immediately won over the fans and developed a wonderfully fruitful partnership with Walker, scoring 16 goals himself and taking the strain off the rest of the attackers.

But McNeill's masterstroke was yet to be pulled. It was known that Aberdeen's young winger Joe Miller was getting increasingly frustrated at Pittodrie. But the Dons had repeatedly said that he was not available to any Scottish club at any price. Alex Ferguson and Kenny Dalglish had made several journeys to watch Miller and it seemed inevitable that he would be the subject of an auction between Manchester United and Liverpool.

Celtic's original inquiry at the start of the season had been rejected, and there the matter appeared to rest. But by November, Aberdeen had changed their minds. McNeill received a telephone call from the Dons' vice-chairman Ian Donald, then with the Scotland team in Bulgaria. Miller could be bought – if the price was right. The price was eventually settled at £650,000; and 48 hours later, Miller was at Parkhead.

What the manager had got was a three-man striking force that would also harry and chase opposition defenders. And because, of all clubs, Celtic had been their first love, McNeill had acquired not only immensely skilful individuals but wholehearted commitment. It was these qualities jointly which allowed Celtic to go all the way to the Championship.

It was not all plain sailing, though. Celtic opened their League programme by losing at Dunfermline, where one of Pat Bonner's few mistakes allowed the Fifers a rare moment of joy in a Premier League campaign which was to end in relegation.

In the course of the season, Celtic were to take seven points out of eight from their Old Firm matches against Rangers. Not only were these important results in shaping up the League, but they were crucial in determining Celtic's attitude. Rangers, the champions, had started the season looking invincible as a result of their spending spree. So it was vital for Celtic to establish an early ascendancy over them on the pitch.

They did so by winning the opening Old Firm game in August, when Stark scored the only goal of the match. They should have done better at Ibrox in November when Rangers Chris Woods and Terry Butcher were sent off along with McAvennie. Celtic, with a man to spare, threw away a two-goal lead and had to settle for a point. But two later wins, at New Year and then in spring, gave them a healthy edge over their oldest rivals.

The club went to the top of the Premier League on 28 November when the leaders Hearts were beaten by Rangers. They were never to be headed again. Rangers fell away badly, and in the last few weeks the only club which could have caught them was Hearts, whom Celtic met on 17 April needing just one point to win the title. That was not to be – as Hearts ran out 2-1 winners. But it did mean that the centenary Championship could be clinched in front of their own supporters seven days later.

The official attendance for the game against Dundee will, in years to come, be quoted as 60,800. Unofficial estimates put the crowd at over 70,000, and they spilled over on to the track all round the ground. But the atmosphere was friendly and no damage was done. Celtic won 3-0, with Morris, who had established himself as one of the real favourites, opening the scoring early in the first half and Walker adding another couple before the end. It meant the Celtic had passed the winning post.

Above *Chris Morris, who McNeill secured from Sheffield Wednesday for a modest £100,000, had a brilliant 1988 European Championship for Eire.*

Below *Mick McCarthy, late of Manchester City, sat out much of his first season at Parkhead with injuries. But he, too, had a fine Euro Championship.*

Parkhead Heroes

Above *Roy Aitken*

Preceding pages *Billy McNeill celebrates victory over Rangers at the end of the 1973 Scottish Cup final.*

Below *Bertie Auld*

Roy Aitken

Roy Aitken, the present Celtic and Scotland captain, looks certain eventually to beat Billy McNeill's post-war record of 486 League games. An inspiring leader by example, Aitken first came into the Celtic side while still a schoolboy at Ardrossan. He made his debut when only 16 in a League Cup-tie against Stenhousemuir and was still at school when he played in his first European tie against Sachsenring Zwickau in East Germany. Equally at home as a central defender or midfield player, Aitken's career has not been short of controversy. He was sent off in the 1984 Scottish Cup final against Aberdeen – but a year later he laid on the winning goal for Frank McGarvey in the final against Dundee United. He does not really deserve the 'hard man' tag, but his driving play and fierce tackling means that he finds it hard to stay out of trouble. National manager Andy Roxburgh appointed him Scotland captain in 1986.

Bertie Auld

With Bobby Murdoch, Auld formed the engine room of the Lisbon Lions. He made his Celtic debut against Hibs in 1957, was transferred to Birmingham City four years later for £15,000, and brought back in 1965 for £12,000 to become one of the club's shrewdest signings. He supplied the cross for John Hughes' goal against Leeds United in the European Cup semi-final of 1970. He won three Scottish Cup medals, three Scottish caps – and played for Hibernian *against* Celtic in the 1972 Cup final. After his retirement he became a successful manager for Partick Thistle.

Pat Bonner

Pat Bonner took over from Peter Latchford as Celtic goalkeeper at the start of the 1980–1 season and played every match that year. His place has been rarely challenged since then, and he became the regular Republic of Ireland goalkeeper. Tall, muscular and strong, he was a key member of the heroic Eire side in the 1988 European Championships – although he had missed that season's Scottish Cup final with a muscle injury. He won his first Scottish Cup-winner's medal in 1985.

Tommy Burns

Skilful, red-headed and above all committed, Tommy Burns has a special affinity with Celtic fans, who judge that if he were not playing, he would be in the Jungle supporting the side. He scored a goal in the infamous European Cup-Winners' Cup tie against Rapide Vienna in 1984 and has earned three Scottish Cup-winner's medals. Only five Celts have played more League games, and he has been capped seven times by Scotland.

Steve Chalmers

Steve Chalmers played 253 League games for Celtic. Centre-forward Chalmers was the top Scottish League scorer in three seasons – 1959–60,

Tommy Burns

1960–1 and 1966–7. He scored the winning goal against Inter Milan in the 1967 European Cup final, which took his total goals tally for that season to 36. His opportunities for Scottich caps were limited, and he played only five games for his country, but he was unquestionably one of the key members of the Lisbon Lions.

John Clark

John Clark broke through in the 1962–3 season and thereafter formed a central defensive partnership with Billy McNeill that was to last throughout his career. Later he became assistant manager at Celtic under McNeill. A meticulous, dour defender, he was just the sort of player needed to underpin the club's flamboyant attacking style. He held his place until the arrival of the mercurial George Connelly and gained four Scottish caps, as well as winning the Scottish Cup three times and the League Cup on five occasions.

Bobby Collins

Bobby Collins was the little winger who went on to become a midfield general. He made his debut for Celtic in the 1949–50 season and was a member of the side which won the Scottish Cup against Motherwell in 1951. His most famous match for Celtic was the 1957–8 League Cup final against Rangers in which he played a big part in that 7–1 hammering. In all, he made 220 appearances for Celtic and won 22 of his 31 caps while he was at the club, before his £25,000 transfer to Everton in 1958.

Only Denis Law and Jimmy McMenemy have had longer Scotland international careers. Collins made his debut against Wales in 1950 and played his last game against Poland in 1965. He orchestrated the Leeds United side that won promotion to the First Division in 1963–4, and became the first Scot to be elected Footballer of the Year in England.

Alfie Conn

Alfie Conn made history when Jock Stein signed him from Tottenham Hotspur in March 1977 at a cost of £65,000: by joining Celtic, the elegant inside forward became the first player to play for both halves of the Old Firm since Alec Bennett joined Rangers from Celtic in 1908. Two months after joining the club, Conn won a Scottish Cup medal against his old team, Rangers – and so became the first man to pick up winner's medals with both clubs. He had scored in Rangers Cup-final victory over Celtic in 1973.

George Connelly

George Connelly first came to the attention of Celtic fans when, still as a schoolboy, he demonstrated his skills at 'keepie-uppie' before a European tie at Parkhead. A cultured sweeper, he had all the talent needed to become one of the all-time Scottish greats. But his frequent walk-outs from the club – and once from a Scotland party – made him a constant headache for Jock Stein. He was still voted Scottish Footballer of the Year in 1973 and won three Scottish Cup-winner's medals to place alongside his Championship successes. He was eventually allowed to leave in 1976 when even Stein's patience with his eccentric star ran out.

Kenny Dalglish

Sean Fallon, Celtic's assistant manager, was kept waiting at the front door of the flat overlooking Ibrox Stadium as he tried to sign a promising teenager. Inside, Kenny Dalglish was busily pulling down pictures of Rangers from the walls.

He was one of the club's best ever signings and one of the unlikeliest because he had never considered Celtic. Once he was a member of the club, however, there was never a more dedicated player.

He joined as a 17-year-old to become a member of a small bunch of youngsters who came to be known as the 'Quality Street Gang': Lou Macari, Danny McGrain and Davie Hay were other members. They became the backbone of the side which replaced the Lisbon Lions and which was to gain the major share of nine successive Championships.

Bobby Collins

Alfie Conn

Unlike many of the other young players whom Stein would coax patiently throughout a couple of seasons in the reserves, Dalglish made his debut in September 1968 in a League Cup-tie against Hamilton – but it was not for two years that he made a first-team place his own. He scored a penalty in his first big match – against Rangers.

By the end of his career at Celtic, in 1975, Dalglish had won every honour in the Scottish game with four Championship medals, four Cup medals and a League Cup medal. He was well on the way to gaining his record 100 caps for Scotland.

He was a very modern player, as comfortable in midfield as he was in his usual striking role. Once asked what his best position was, Stein replied: 'Och, just let him on the park.' Dalglish had an insatiable appetite for the game and could often be found training on his own or with the ground staff

Above *George Connelly*

Left *Kenny Dalglish*

63

boys in the afternoon when all the other players had long since gone home. Billy McNeill acted as his mentor.

It was his ambition to reach the very heights in football and after those seven seasons, he realised that it was necessary for him to go to England to achieve that aim. The Celtic side was beginning to break up, the long period of success was coming to an end and even Stein realised that he could not hold on to his brightest star.

He began a second career at Liverpool, replacing Kevin Keegan, who went to Hamburg. In 1985 he became manager at Anfield – after winning every honour open to him. His only regret must be that he never had a European triumph while he was at Celtic. But he had everything else.

John ('Dixie') Deans

It says much for the character of Dixie Deans that even his famous penalty-decider miss against Inter Milan in the semi-final of the European Cup in 1972 could not stop him from becoming the most popular Celtic player of his time. A chunky centre forward with an irrepressible sense of humour, Deans was signed from Motherwell with a chronic disciplinary problem which Jock Stein overcame. Three weeks after that penalty miss, he made amends with a hat-trick against Hibs in the biggest Cup final win of the century. He played twice for Scotland.

Dixie Deans

Jimmy Delaney

Jimmy Delaney was the best-loved Celtic player of his era, a winger who could torment defences and a man able to score important goals. His arrival at the club in 1935 – for a £20 signing-on fee and a wage of £3 a week – was the start of better times for Celtic, who won the Championship in 1936 and the Scottish Cup a year later. In 1938, he was a member of the Celtic side that won the Empire Exhibition Cup – an unofficial British Championship – by beating Everton 1–0 in the Final.

He broke his arm so badly in 1939 that the surgeon said that, if Delaney had not been a footballer, he would have been obliged to amputate it. The war interrupted his career, but he still gained 13 Scottish Caps. He will be remembered for scoring the only goal against England in the 1946 Victory International at Hampden Park. Weeks before, he had become Matt Busby's first signing for Manchester United and he played in the side which beat Blackpool in the 1948 Cup Final. He continued playing until 1956, finishing with Elgin City in the Highland League.

Johnny Doyle

Johnny Doyle had a tragically brief career with Celtic. The winger was signed from Ayr United in 1976 for £90,000 but was hampered by injury. He was the man sent off in the League decider against Rangers in 1979 – so providing the chance for the other 10 to win a famous victory. He played in the 1980 Cup-winning side. But in 1982 he died after electrocuting himself by accident at home. When Celtic won the League that year, the fans continuously chanted his name.

Bobby Evans

Bobby Evans held Celtic together during a long, difficult passage of the club's history. Without the advantage of either the League Cup for some of his career or European football for the entire length of it, he still managed to play more games for Celtic than anyone apart from Billy McNeill, Danny McGrain and Roy Aitken.

His career stretches from immediately after World War 2 until his transfer to Chelsea in 1960, when his place was starting to be challenged by McNeill. His 385 League performances were models of consistency, in whatever position the club used him.

In that period Celtic won the Championship only once – in 1954 – so Evans had to guide a succession of sides which rarely aspired to the sort of quality their supporters expected. But there was never any doubt about his own commitment and skill.

An edgy, sensitive man off the field, he was honest when on it. In his long Celtic career he was only twice cautioned, and on one of those occasions it was for protesting to a referee after the match was over. He won two Cup medals, but his worth was probably better judged by his Scotland statistics. Evans played for his country 48 times, despite occasionaly being dropped. That was only five caps short of the 53 which George Young set as a Scotland record. He twice captained Scotland against England.

He left Celtic under something of a cloud, and went to Chelsea before returning to Scotland as player-manager of Third Lanark. He was almost 40 when he retired in 1967.

Sean Fallon

Opposite *Willie Fernie*

Sean Fallon

No-one could have made a more inauspicious debut for Celtic than Sean Fallon. Signed for £5,000 from Glenavon on March 27, 1950, he put through his own net after only 34 minutes of his first game. But that did not stop him from going on to forge a 10-year career with the club. His determination caught the imagination of the fans as a rugged player either at left back or on the left wing. He became a great favourite of the club chairman Robert Kelly and was made captain. When injured, he handed the captaincy to Jock Stein – for whom he became assistant manager during all the glory years of the '60s and '70s.

Willie Fernie

Willie Fernie had a style and grace which made him the favourite Celt of all those fans who savoured the finer skills. He played 219 games for the club and was largely responsible for Celtic winning the League Cup final in 1957. Soon after, he was sold to Middlesbrough for £17,500. At centre forward, or later at wing half, he would glide effortlessly past opponents and never seemed to have a hair out of place. He won 12 caps for Scotland and was a member of the 1954 World Cup squad. A brief return to Celtic from England was not a success as by now the relaxed subtleties of his game clashed with the faster modern style. He was later manager of Kilmarnock.

Patsy Gallacher

Robert Kelly described him as 'the greatest player I have ever seen.' He was painfully thin and looked as if he could be easily knocked off the ball. But he was the best dribbler of his day, a proven goalscorer and an all round athlete. He made his debut in 1911 and six months later scored one of the goals which gave Celtic a Scottish Cup victory over Clyde.

   He scored one of the most astonishing of all Scottish Cup final goals in 1925 against Dundee, dribbling past defender after defender until he was knocked down. But he jammed the ball between his feet and then somersaulted into the net with it!

   When Gallacher joined Celtic, the team which had taken six successive League titles had broken up. Inspired by this slight figure, Celtic went on to win four titles in a row. He played 13 times for Eire and ended up with four Scottish Cup medals and seven Championship medals. His achievements and his style place him among the three or four finest inside forwards ever to grace the Scottish League.

Tommy Gemmell

Tommy Gemmell

It was Tommy Gemmell's shot which transformed the European Cup final of 1967 against Inter Milan and crowned a season that changed the course of Celtic's history. A brash extrovert of a full back, Gemmell was amongst the first of the 'overlappers' who influenced the game in the '60s. 'Remember you're a full back first,' Stein would tell him. He also had the distinction of scoring Celtic's only goal in the 1970 European Cup final against Feyenoord; while his last-minute effort against Kilmarnock the year before had brought Celtic a fourth successive title. He won 18 caps for Scotland, either as a left

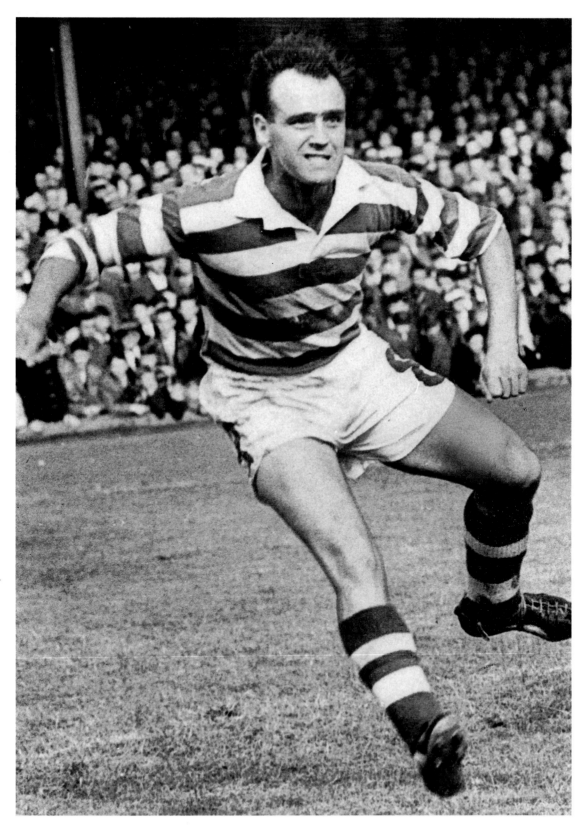

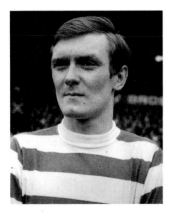

Davie Hay

back or a right back. Nicknamed 'Danny Kaye' because of his facial resemblence to the actor, he was always a free spirit. He ended his career with Nottingham Forest, then went into management with Dundee and, later, Albion Rovers.

Davie Hay

Davie Hay looked like a winner when he entered the first team during the 1969–70 season, and he went on to play in both the Scottish Cup final and the European Cup final. Celtic lost both – possibly an omen for his career.

Although he won five Championship medals and two Cup medals, starting out as a full back and becoming a midfield player, he was best remembered at that time for his Scotland role in the 1974 World Cup, where he was the inspiration of the unbeaten side in West Germany. Shortly afterwards, he was transferred to Chelsea for £225,000, but eye trouble led to an early end to his career in 1979. He won 27 Scottish caps. He became manager of Motherwell and was called back to Celtic as boss; but his reign was an uneasy one and it ended when he was sacked to make way for Billy McNeill's return to the club.

Mo Johnston

John Hughes

John Hughes was known as 'Yogi' to the fans. Big, strong, fast – and totally erratic – he was Celtic's 'nearly man'. He made his debut in the 1960–1 season, but his inconsistent form meant that he was always prone to being dropped. That was the case in the 1967 European Cup final. His most important goal came three years later in the second leg of the European Cup Final against Leeds United at Hampden Park, when he equalised Billy Bremner's opening goal and set Celtic on course for victory. He was transferred, along with Willie Wallace, to Crystal Palace in 1971. His 116 goals makes him one of only four Celtic players to pass the century since the war.

Mo Johnston

Mo Johnston was signed from Watford in October 1984. Many fans felt that the club should have bought him 12 months earlier, when he went to England from Partick Thistle for only £100,000. A consistent goalscorer, especially from close range, he scored the third goal on the day that Celtic beat St Mirren to clinch the Championship in 1986. At the end of the 1986–7 season he left to join the French club Nantes, one of a growing army of British players seeking their fortunes on the continental stage.

Jimmy Johnstone

Jock Stein was once asked what was the greatest contribution he had made to Celtic. Pondering long and hard, he replied: 'I think that keeping Jimmy Johnstone in the game for so long was the best thing I ever did.

Johnstone was one of the last old-fashioned wingers. He could dribble, feint past opponents and was a shrewd crosser of the ball. His gifts were supreme. Often, he seemed to want to beat defenders not once but three or

Jimmy Johnstone

four times. And then, just when his critics were pointing out that he had snared himself in one of his mazy dribbles, he would emerge – the ball seemingly glued to his toe-caps – to deliver a scoring pass to his strikers.

On the other hand, his temperament was suspect. All too often in the early stages of his career, crude and heavy tackling was the only defence against his wizardry. That always risked rousing the winger's quick, fierce temper. It was part of Stein's genius that, in later years, Johnstone was only infrequently at odds with the authorities.

His most famous match was the European Cup semi-final against Leeds United in 1970 when, over two legs, he taunted England full-back Terry Cooper to the edge of despair. He kept Cooper, a fine overlapping full-back, pinned into his own corner of the field and one of Leeds' best tactics was nullified.

'He's not a bad lad with regard to being against authority,' Stein said. 'It's just that if there is any trouble, he always seems to be in the thick of it.

He was twice suspended for a week by Celtic in his early years and later, in 1974, he was involved in the notorious incident at Largs before the World Cup when coast guards had to be called out as a dawn trip in a rowing boat almost ended calamitously. Two days later his fine play helped Scotland to beat England at Hampden Park. It was Johnstone's own reply to the barrage of criticism.

He hated flying. In 1968, he was promised by Stein that he would not have to go to Belgrade for a European Cup-tie – just as long as he helped Celtic gain a four-goal lead in the first leg. He did just that.

In 1976, Johnstone was given a testimonial, in conjunction with Bobby Lennox, against Manchester United. When it was over, the winger walked across to Parkhead's Jungle, where his most enthusiastic supporters always stood, and he threw his boots to them as a souvenir. He was treasured for the way he played, and for what he was – a unique footballer.

Bobby Lennox

Bobby Lennox

In a career which stretched from 1962 to 1980, Bobby Lennox not only played in 296 League games (and in 50 others as a substitute) but became the club's leading post-war scorer with 168 goals. He played in the 1967 European Cup-winning team, and in domestic competitions was an ever-present as Celtic won nine League championships in a row, as well as five Scottish Cups and five League Cups. A speedy winger, he lost little of his pace as the years rolled by. Under-used by Scotland, for whom he won only 10 caps, he scored a goal against England in 1967 in a 3–2 victory, the first defeat for the World Cup winners on their own soil. He is still a member of the Celtic back-room staff.

Lou Macari

Lou Macari

Lou Macari, an elusive striker, was one of a bunch of talented youngsters who were the natural heirs to the Lisbon Lions, and was expected to have a distinguished career with Celtic. In fact, it did not turn out that way: Macari started only 50 League matches for the club; but he was a member of the side which won the Scottish Cup in 1971 and 1972. The following year he was transferred to Manchester United for £200,000. On his retirement he went into management, making a successful career at Swindon Town. Macari won a total of 24 Scottish caps, six of them while at Parkhead.

Following pages *Jimmy Johnstone – close control at speed.*

Frank McAvennie

Another of Billy McNeill's signings when he returned as manager in 1987. The tall and bustling McAvennie was the perfect foil for Andy Walker. Signed for £850,000 from West Ham United, whom he had joined from St Mirren, McAvennie immediately started putting the ball in the net, ending the season triumphantly by scoring the two goals in the Cup Final by which Celtic beat Dundee United. He was a member of Scotland's World Cup squad in Mexico in 1986.

Brian McClair

Brian McClair was Celtic's leading goalscorer in the four seasons he spent with the club. He joined them as the replacement for Charlie Nicholas at the start of the 1983–4 season, in which he led the League with 23 goals. He was substitute in the Cup final team of 1985 and scored one of the goals against St Mirren which clinched the Championship on the last day of the next season. At the end of 1986–7, he took advantage of freedom of contract to join Manchester United, with a tribunal fixing the fee at approximately £750,000.

Brian McClair

Frank McGarvey

Billy McNeill set a Scottish transfer record when he signed Frank McGarvey from Liverpool for £250,000 in March 1980. Two months later he had won the first of his Scottish Cup medals. A bustling centre-forward who could usually be relied on to score more than 20 goals a season, he had five successful years at Celtic, where he was the perfect foil for Charlie Nicholas. Days after scoring the winning goal in the 1985 Scottish Cup final against Dundee United, he was transferred to St Mirren for only £70,000 after refusing a new pay deal. Capped seven times for Scotland, he won a Cup Winner's medal with St Mirren in 1987 after scoring their winner in the semi-final against Hearts.

Danny McGrain

Danny McGrain fought courageously against illness and injury to establish himself as one of the greatest full-backs ever to play for Celtic and Scotland. Few players have had to overcome so many problems.

He signed for the club in 1967 and made his debut three years later. But in 1972 at Brockville against Falkirk, he fractured his skull in an accidental clash. After treatment he carried on but complained of dizziness at half-time and fainted in the tunnel. He regained consciousness only later that evening in hospital. But he went on to make a complete recovery.

He made his Scotland debut against Wales in 1973 and, injuries aside, held it for nine years – but not without pain. After the 1974 World Cup, he felt tired and put it down to the draining effects of a long season. But the condition was later diagnosed as diabetes and it could be controlled only by daily injections of insulin. This became part of his life.

Again his career was threatened by an ankle injury which kept him out of the 1978 World Cup. For months no-one could diagnose what was wrong.

Frank McGarvey